More Praise of Renessa Boley Layne...

"The Fast Lane, Wrong Direction message is important for students entering college and is even more critical as they exit and launch their professional careers. I hired Renessa to speak at our graduate and PhD retreat, as well as coach a top-performing mentee. We were so impressed that she's already in the budget for next year!"

—DR. CONSTINIA CHARBONNETTE, Director of Recruitment, Fellowship and Life, West Virginia University

"Our leadership program participants benefited greatly from Renessa's session on career management. Her energy, expertise and ability to engage the audience was fantastic. Participants left seeing new ways to move their career forward and setting actions for themselves."

—DELONTE EATON, Learning and Development Specialist, DC Water

"Renessa's talk to the Georgetown students was fantastic! I learned how to project more confidence, to build quick rapport and strategically engage the people that I talk to. I put every one of your tips into action the very same week, and as a result, I stood out among my peers in a very intense interview process for a fellowship. The best part—I got the fellowship! Thanks again!"

—AYESHA IBRAHIM, student, Georgetown University School of Nursing and Health Studies

FAST LANE
Wrong Direction

Insider Secrets College Grads Must Master
to Succeed in Career and Life.

RENESSA BOLEY LAYNE

Designer Life Unlimited LLC
Oakland, California U.S.A.

Fast Lane, Wrong Direction
*Insider Secrets College Grads Must Master
to Succeed in Career and Life.*
Copyright ©2016 Renessa Boley Layne

ISBN-13: Softcover 978-0983335566
ISBN-10: Softcover 0983335567

Cover artwork copyright ©2016 by T.L. Price
Editing and composition by Dennis Tuttle, 5editorial, Silver Spring, Md.

All rights reserved. No part of this book may be reproduced or transmitted in any form or by any means, electronic or mechanical, including photocopying, recording, or by any information storage and retrieval system, without permission in writing from the copyright owner.

This book was printed in the United States of America.

10 9 8 7 6 5 4 3 2 1

For bulk or promotional copies of this book, contact:
 www.designerlifeunlimited.com

Also order this book online through:
 www.amazon.com
 www.barnesandnoble.com

To all young dreamers who want the most out of life. . . .

Contents

Introduction: New Game, New Rules   9

Section 1: Design Your Success   15

Section 2: This Ain't No Fairy Tale   27

Section 3: Hugs & Handshakes   37

Section 4: Your Competitive Edge   53

Section 5: Fundamentals of Turning Pro   73

Section 6: Bonus Secret—Measuring Up   83

Section 7: You've Got a Rep to Protect   91

Section 8: Top of Your Game   103

Section 9: Go Big or Go Home   115

Section 10: Milk Your Age For All It's Worth   129

Section 11: Happiness Matters   141

Closing: It's Just a Game   151

"Your life is like a basketball game;
the tempo keeps changing."
— Michael Jordan, basketball Hall of Famer

INTRODUCTION
••••
New Game, New Rules

SUCCEEDING IN YOUR internship, your first real job or a new business is no longer about academics and book smarts. Whether you know it or not, the game of success is about to change for you–fast. If you're approaching graduation or getting your first taste of the professional workplace, you must realize that you're turning pro. You're moving from the amateurs to the big leagues, and you're embarking on a new game with a new set of rules. If you don't know the rules, you'll find yourself in the fast lane going in the wrong direction.

And that's why I wrote this book.

I was one of those achievers—in the fast lane going in the wrong direction—at the start of my career. I looked very successful on the outside. I earned a six-figure salary in my 20s, I was a key contributor to a firm, but I was bored, burned out, unfulfilled and not nearly as fired up about adulthood as I thought I would be. I graduated with an engineering degree from Stanford University, and while I did many things right at the start of my career, I did other things really, really wrong.

It's not uncommon for young professionals to stumble through the early years, working really hard at the wrong goals, missing out on ideal opportunities, getting passed over for promotion or feeling inexplicably insecure about whether you're headed in the right or wrong direction. You look like a pro but deep down inside you don't feel like one.

Often, you look around and think everyone else has it all together and you are the only one who didn't get the memo on what the heck you're supposed to do with this thing called work and life! Truth is, you're not alone. Most of your peers are in some version of "wrong direction" themselves—either they just don't know it yet or won't admit it. With this book in hand, however, that does not have to be you.

Perhaps you are already in the fast lane. You've got big dreams and you're optimistic you can make those dreams come true. You believe in making a meaningful difference in the world. You believe in bucking the system and finding better, faster ways to do just about everything. You want a lot out of life and you're willing to take risks, though secretly you're scared shirtless and haven't a clue what's next. It's all good. I won't tell anybody.

While you may agree that you're in the fast lane, how would you know if you're in the fast lane going in the wrong direction?

Then, again, perhaps "fast lane" is an overstatement for you. You might consider yourself a late bloomer, scrambling just to figure out where you are and what you want to do with your life. Maybe you've made some poor choices in the past and are trying to make up for lost time. That's okay. These principles apply to you, too, and will equip you to turn around your success in no time.

Whether you're in the fast lane, slow lane or somewhere in between, you must realize that "wrong direction" can take many forms. One way is that our destination can be off; we can be in the wrong major, wrong career or wrong business. Even though I studied engineering, the truth is I didn't like math and I hated science. The problem was that I was good at both. I was black, I was a young woman, and mentors advised me to take advantage of the opportunities brought by the need for greater diversity in STEM (science, technology, engineering and mathematics) fields, so off I went in pursuit of an engineering degree.

The summer before my freshman year, I was interning for a major technology company when my mentor asked me what I wanted to do with my career.

I answered emphatically, "I want to work on a fashion magazine!"

The confusion on his face reflected what I would say to myself each day: "Really, Renessa? And that's why you're here, building file servers and inserting motherboards? Really?"

No.

The real reason was that engineering internship provided a full-tuition scholarship to Stanford, a guaranteed internship each summer and a guaranteed post-graduation job. If a company was willing to do all that for a military kid from a little town in Alabama whose teenage parents were barely 17 when she was born, then I would be anything they wanted me to be—gladly. That's why I was building file servers and inserting motherboards, and that's why the fashion magazine artwork was under the bed.

I was hopelessly bored with that job, and even then things deep inside felt a little off. But for a teenager making more money than my mother on a summer job, they sure "looked" right! I couldn't articulate it at the time, but I had this fear my "right" decisions weren't going to turn out so right. It's kind of the same feeling we have when we pinpoint the first dude to get whacked in a horror movie: We all know it's coming, but we have to let the scene play out. Deep down, I feared I would be successful, but not particularly *happy*. Nonetheless, I convinced myself that a hefty engineering paycheck would make up for the boredom I felt inside.

I was in the fast lane going in the wrong direction already.

Maybe you can relate to my story. Maybe you're studying a major you couldn't be less interested in, but you have invested so much time already that you should see it through. Maybe you're applying to a graduate program because your parents, professors or mentors think it's best, yet the voice in your head is whispering, "train wreck." Or maybe you've had your first taste of practical work in your field and, to your dismay, you're already looking for your "Get Out of Jail Free" card for more meaningful work. It's like, "What the $#:@*&! and why didn't anybody warn me it could be like this?!?!"

If any of these scenarios ring true, you might be in the fast lane going in the wrong direction.

But hold up! Wrong direction isn't just about the wrong destination. *How* you pursue your success from here forward is equally as important as *what* you pursue. You could be in the right career, working for the right company, building the right business—and still find yourself miserable, insecure, anxious, scared and frustrated. That is also wrong direction. How you go after your big dreams will make all the difference on how happy you'll feel and how smooth your ride will be along the way. It will determine how quickly you get promoted, who will open doors for you, and what opportunities come your way.

"Fast lane, *right* direction" is the lesson they don't teach in the college career center workshops.

When I wrote the first *Fast Lane, Wrong Direction Professional Edition*, I had no thought of writing a second version of the book for young adults. But over time, I received more and more invitations to speak about this topic to college students and young professionals, and I quickly realized the dangers of "wrong direction" show up for all of us, no matter the age.

College students and young professionals grapple with the same questions of achievement, fulfillment, insecurity, direction and choices as the established professionals I coach every day; the conversations just sound a little different. Most of us "old heads" wish we had more people in our lives when we were your age to make sense of the questions, feelings and decisions we were making at this critical starting point in our professional careers. We wanted to know when to speed up, when to slow down, when to speak and when to shut up in the pursuit of our goals.

I have interviewed countless professionals and entrepreneurs from all over the world who found themselves in the fast lane going in the wrong direction at some point as they were turning pro. I asked them what advice they would give the 21-year-old version of themselves to find and maintain *right* direction.

This book is our advice to you.

These are literally the insider secrets—the strategies, mindset and principles—established professionals wish they knew at the start of their careers on how to do work they love and truly thrive in it. These are the hidden secrets that convert internships to full-time job offers and catapult you leaps and bounds beyond your peers in the workplace. More than that, these insider secrets will help you actually enjoy the ride on the road to success.

You'll learn soon enough that I like to keep things real, so the lessons and wisdom here will do absolutely nothing for you if you do nothing with it. But if you're smart enough to apply what you learn in this book, there is no limit to what you can achieve, experience and enjoy in your work and life right now.

"If you don't build your dream,
someone will hire you to help build theirs."
— Tony Gaskins, motivational speaker

SECTION 1
••••
Design Your Success

MANY YOUNG PEOPLE fall into the trap of relying on others to plan out their lives–their parents, their academic advisors, their bosses. The reality is that success in your career, business and overall life starts and ends with *numero uno*.

Yeah, that's right… you.

Owning this reality is crucial as you embark on your next role, whether it's an internship, fellowship or your first professional job. For some, this role will be an incredibly valuable experience, one you'll look back on years from now and recognize as a pivotal moment in your career or business trajectory. It might solidify your major, change your graduate study or open the door for a totally unexpected and exciting professional adventure. For others, you'll look back at this time and wonder, "What was the point of it all?"

At best, you might view your internship or your first jobs as a colossal waste of time, or, at worse, a clear indication of just how "wrong direction" you were in your life. The difference between this being the best of times or worst of times for you will hinge on one major skill…

… Your ability to design your success.

Designing your success is the first section of this book because it is so difficult to carve the perfect path, as if there is such a thing. I coach people who are 10, 20, even 30 years into their careers and it's not uncommon for folks to find themselves in jobs they hate and lifestyles they don't want. They often appear successful on the outside. They may even be six- and seven-figure earners, but often they're bored, burned out, unfulfilled and have no idea how to fix things.

I used to be that way (minus the "30 years into their career" claim), and I'm hell-bent on ensuring that's not the case for you! And it won't be the case for you if you begin to master the habit of designing your success.

Designing your success doesn't mean you have to know exactly what you want to do with your life long-term nor does it mean you must control all the outcomes of your internship or job. What it does mean, however, is that you develop a clearer idea of what you *think* you may want to experience in your life and career, then take the deliberate and strategic actions required to make that desire a reality. You're not passively waiting for someone to instruct you on who you should be, what program you should apply for, and exactly what to do to succeed in it. You're not holding your breath, hoping someone notices your hard work and extends a full-time offer to you at the end of the summer.

Instead, you're mapping out your own goals, sharing those goals with advisors you value—your boss, parents, professors, mentors, etc.—and soliciting their input, wisdom, direction, resources and clarity on how to achieve the success you want. As you do that, life will give you feedback, positively and sometimes negatively, to instruct you on what to do and where to go next. That's how it works.

Success after college begins first with a *design*, and this next section will start you on your way to creating yours.

INSIDER SECRET #1
Passion Matters

"Your work is going to fill a large part of your life, and the only way to be truly satisfied is to do what you believe is great work."
—STEVE JOBS, Apple Inc. co-founder and CEO

One of the most common questions young people ask themselves takes one of these two forms:

What is my passion or purpose?
— or —
How do I get paid for it?

The answers to these two questions are vitally important because they dictate how much money you will make on the job, how fast you are promoted, the impact you will make in your field and the amount of joy, freedom and fulfillment you'll experience in the process. Each of these—money, promotion, impact and fulfillment—is something that we *earn*. But contrary to what most of us have been taught, we don't earn it solely by virtue of what school we went to or how hard we work.

What binds all of the above together is passion. Passion matters. It matters when deciding what course to major in and what course to audit. It matters when considering whether or not to attend grad school. It matters when determining how to evaluate your internship and which full-time job offer to take. Passion matters, and making the decision to pursue passion is insider secret #1.

There are countless stories of people who have done all the right things to secure an outward appearance of success yet completely miss the boat on the vitality and juice that comes from a life of passion. They didn't just wake up one day and decide to start faking it. Some had a gnawing sense of dissatisfaction at about your age; they just didn't know what to do about it. Others started off in the right direction toward their career and business dreams—all fired up—but the inevitable failures, setbacks and bad decisions we all experience along the way discouraged them and ultimately squashed their vision.

For a while, that was me.

When I started on the engineering track, I did so for the wrong reasons. I wasn't designing my *own* life. I was designing my mentor's life, the female geek role model's dream. The purely technical route wasn't a bad dream to have, but it wasn't for me, so I needed to figure out what was my right direction. I was very analytical, which played well to science, technology and engineering fields, but my most natural skill set was in communicating through speaking, writing and graphics, and I was far more fascinated by people than I was things. Maybe I could work in a technical field, but in a different role?

I didn't know, but I was at least willing to take the risk and try new things to figure it out. All these years later, it turns out I'm still a geek, but in a different way that suits me perfectly. I now use my analytical abilities to speak, write and create products that help people, a lot of whom are engineers, to strategically design their most luscious life ever!

Sweet!

What I learned over time was that the greatest act of gratitude for my life was to live it to the absolute fullest, to figure out what I was put on earth to do—what juiced and excited *me*. That sweet spot is where I would be most successful, earn the most money and do the most good in the world.

Some kids grow up being told about all the things they can't achieve. Others grow up being told, "You can be anything you want to be!" I disagree with both perspectives. You have a calling in your life, a personal destiny, a job to do in this world, and your passions leave clues to that call, which can take multiple forms across your lifetime. But just because somebody says you'll never amount to anything does not make it so. Any one of numerous forks in the road can change your entire life, from where you live, where you work, who you meet or marry—to how you grow, mature and become the person you are destined to be. One thing is almost for certain: you will *not* be the same person you are today in five years, 10 years, 20 years.

In the same vein, just because daddy says you should be a lawyer, developer or accountant doesn't make it so, either. Sure, you can try it, but if law or construction or accounting is not your "thing," you're going to blow it. Or worse yet, you'll end up busting your butt to achieve someone else's dreams while sporting an imaginary "life sucks" sticker on your forehead because you're miserable doing so.

Some people come out of the womb with passion written all over them. They're like Michael Phelps, Ryan Seacrest, and, oh, that dorm mate who knew she wanted to be a doctor at age five! Those are the lucky souls.

And then there are the rest of us, just trying to get a clue, hoping to God we can figure out how to get paid for this degree before student loan repayment kicks in!

My friend Joey and I were having a discussion about passion and I was fascinated by what he shared:

"When you start talking about being aligned with your passion, I think some people would be scared by that because they don't know what their passion is. They might get caught in a loop of 'I need to figure out my passion before I can do anything,' and that's a really dangerous place to be. I'm somewhat of a believer in 'What's my passion for now?'

"I think trying on different passions like you would try on different outfits is a good thing. It's the passion for the time. It's the willingness to be authentic, the willingness to say, 'I'm not exactly sure.' How many times do people in the fast lane say, 'You know, I'm not sure?' Sometimes we must get comfortable with the fact that we don't know the answer. If someone could get to the point where they say, 'I don't know what my life purpose is, but for now the thing I'm committed and focused on is this, this, and this." If, at the core, you're willing to be real and authentic, then the other stuff tends to sort itself out."

Before I graduated college, like Joey, I tried on different "outfits" in search of my passion. I knew the purely technical track wasn't for me, but I was committed to earning that engineering degree because I didn't have a clue what else to do. To help figure it out, I did a summer internship selling *Cover Girl* cosmetics for Procter & Gamble in Atlanta, I modeled in San Francisco and did a management consulting internship in New York City. Even when I started working and was making great money on my job, I enrolled in interior design classes at night, all in search of my "thing."

Career clarity didn't happen right away. I did a few jobs I didn't like to get a clue on what I did like. That was okay because knowing what "ain't it" is as important as knowing what is. Passion is a matter of the heart, and when it comes to passionate work, you'll know it when you find it. So keep looking until you do.

INSIDER SECRET #2
Intersection Between Your Passion and Marketplace

"I wasn't fully convinced that you could draw pictures and get paid to do so. Yet in my advertising business, that's essentially what I do."
—JOEY COLEMAN, Chief Experience Composer, Design Symphony

The obvious question for all of us when it comes to doing meaningful work is, "How the heck do I get paid for this?" Understandably, this question doesn't apply if your passion is a hobby, pastime or an old sport you have no intention of ever getting paid for. But if you want to connect your passion to a paycheck or if you're in a company doing X work but want to figure out how you can do Y work within that same company, you must find the intersection between your passion and the marketplace.

But what does that mean and how do you do it? How do you find an internship or new job that can move you closer to doing work you love? For well over 10 years, the answer to that question completely eluded me, and through that old-fashioned school of hard knocks, I began to figure it out. When trying to find that sweet spot between your passions and the marketplace, where checks get cut and your bank account grows, you must make three commitments:

1.) Get real about your passions;
2.) Pay attention to your talents and skills;
3.) Understand what the marketplace wants.

I will unpack each of these commitments separately in the next three chapters so that you understand how crucial they are to designing your success. But for now, just know there is an intersection between your passion and the marketplace, and finding that intersection is how you'll get paid to do the work you enjoy.

INSIDER SECRET #3
Get Real About Your Passions

"One of the huge mistakes people make is they try to force an interest on themselves. You don't choose your passions; your passions choose you."
—JEFF BEZOS, chairman and CEO, Amazon

To find the intersection between your passion and a paycheck, you must get beyond the abstract idea that "passion matters" and discover your *own* passions. I'm not saying you have to figure out your passion right away; there's absolutely nothing wrong if you feel clueless in this moment. Nor am I suggesting that every job you work will be a job you're passionate about. Sometimes, you will have to do things you don't like to get your foot in the door, to learn a necessary skill, or to merely survive. But if doing meaningful work is important to you, eventually figuring out your true passions is key.

The first step to identifying passion is to get real about what you like. You won't believe how challenging that is for some young people or the myriad of lies they will tell themselves to keep from owning up to what they really want! Some worry what their parents, teachers or friends will think of their passion, especially if they've invested so much time, energy and expense going down one path only to switch to another. Others question whether their passion has any real value in the marketplace. I mean, we can universally agree that being a doctor who saves lives is crucially important, but baking cupcakes? Not so much, right?

Wrong!

Sophie LaMontagne and Katherine Kallinis, stars of the TV show "DC Cupcakes," were signed by the TLC cable network to do an entire reality show dedicated to…

(drumroll please)… *baking cupcakes*. It doesn't matter whether you value baking cupcakes or not, some cable network valued their passion and talent enough to give them their own show.

I launched an online course titled *First Steps to Love Your Work: How to Discover, Design and Do Work You Love,* and in this program I show people how to identify what they're passionate about, connect that to their talents and take the immediate steps to begin to make money doing what they enjoy. I warn people in that program that if you don't get honest about what you really want to do or be, you set yourself up to chase "false positives," pursuits that you've convinced yourself are your passions because they are realistic or "acceptable" pursuits when they really don't satisfy you—and never will. I was so guilty of that in my 20s.

Two things I can promise about passion, destiny, purpose and all its synonyms: It will take courage to find your passion but you will know when it speaks to your heart. It may take a little more time for some, and people might not always "get" you as you're figuring things out. But if you have the courage to find your "right direction" and stay true to it, your passion will feel like the most natural, congruent truth in the world. And the only fear you will feel is whether you have what it takes to accomplish what you want, but deep down you will know if it's the mountain you were born to climb.

INSIDER SECRET #4
Pay Attention to Your Talents and Strengths

"Don't bring your need to the marketplace, bring your skill."
—JIM ROHN, entrepeneur and motivational speaker

Best-selling author, teacher and counselor John Eldredge wrote, "Desire reveals design, and design reveals destiny." What this means is that if you evaluate your passions (those are your desires), you will find that you have some innate skills and talents that support that desire (which is your design).

As you enhance your skills over time through instruction, practice and experience, you are effectively mastering your design. As you master your design, you will ultimately reach your destiny—the manifestation of your passion in the form of a job, business, or service that benefits people around you.

Take a tiger for example. Its desire is to hunt and kill. Every part of the tiger's design supports that desire: its paws are padded for stealth, its fur is colored for camouflage, its jaws can crush a human with one bite, and its body is built for speed and strength. Its design perfectly equips the tiger as a powerful hunter, which is consistent with its desire.

Notice, however, that a tiger does not fly.

It has no desire to fly, nor is it designed to fly. That is why… a tiger does not fly! The same is the case with you. Put aside your fear for one moment and take stock of what you really want to do in your life. Notice how your design—your talents, your temperament, and your experiences (both good and bad)—all support that desire.

As you begin designing your own success, your responsibility is to get a clear picture of the skills you need to accomplish what you want, the skills you currently possess and the skills you lack. Have a gazillion conversations with people who have done what you want to do. The "people-who-have-done-what-you-want-to-do" part is key. (That's a "writer-downer" for those of you taking notes or highlighting on an e-reader!)

So often we seek advice from people who haven't a clue how to achieve what *we* want and wonder why we feel so confused. If you don't know anyone who has accomplished something similar in the field of your passion, ask around. Ask friends, colleagues, mentors, bosses, parents. Somebody knows somebody who can help you piece together your path.

A favorite proverb of mine reads, "A man's gift makes room for him, and brings him before great men." In the marketplace, your gift is your talent. Maximize your talent in line with your passion and watch the masterpiece of your life begin to unfold.

INSIDER SECRET #5
Understand What the Market Wants

"Don't ask yourself what the world needs; ask yourself what makes you come alive. And then go do that. Because what the world needs is people who have come alive."
—HOWARD THURMAN, author, theologian and civil rights leader

Understanding what the marketplace wants *and is willing to pay for* is where many new grads fall short in designing their success. I can't think of anything you could possibly want to do with your life for which there is not a demand in some company or organization somewhere; you simply have to find what and where the demand is and what form it takes.

eBay was built by a man wanting to sell off items around his house. There's a woman on the Internet making over $100,000 a year selling home-study programs—for quilting! A colleague earns a ton of money teaching people how to become basketball referees. Believe it or not, some dude wrote a book called *The Art of Mackin'* and created a high-end coaching program to teach men how to become "players and macks." It's ridiculous, but there's a market for such a thing and this guy understands what his market wants.

The opening quote by Howard Thurman might seem to contradict the title of this chapter when, in actuality, it supports the chapter perfectly. To design your own success, you must *first* ask yourself what makes *you* come alive. What are *you* passionate about? The next step is to find the demand in the marketplace for what you want to do, whether it's entrepreneurial in nature or job-related.

My friend Lauren Solomon is an image consultant based in Los Angeles. The road to her business was a prime example of finding the intersection of your passion and the marketplace. The inspiration to start image consulting came about when she was taking an executive MBA program. She was working for a prominent bank in New York and the idea came to her as part of a marketing assignment to create her ideal job. When presented with the assignment, she recalls:

"I didn't know what it would be, but there had to be something out there. The only thing I loved to do was what I did for my friends when they were getting married—advising them on their hair, styling them, etc. I loved doing things that made people smile. So, I went to class and presented image consulting for executives. I asked the question of the class, 'Is this something you might need?' All the hands shot up."

Once Lauren got an inkling of validation that the marketplace would want a version of what was still a pretty ill-defined passion, she had to piece her way through the next steps, taking whatever courses were available and seeking the advice of the few people who were pioneering the industry. Image consulting was not an established profession at the time.

"I had been practicing what I was learning with my teammates at the bank," she said. "I'd get people to buy me lunch in exchange for a haircut. I would bring in fabrics, eyeglasses, etc. My team was a motley crew within the bank and some of the

> ## *Conversations in the Fast Lane*
> ### *... on Designing Your Success.*
>
> ✓ Are you clear today on the things you are passionate about? If so, how are you using that knowledge to find work you enjoy?
>
> ✓ If not, what steps can you take to get a better idea? Who can advise you and what resources can help?
>
> ✓ Are you confident about your passions or are you afraid to acknowledge what you really want to do with your life?
>
> ✓ How do your talents and strengths (your design) align to your passions (your desire)? Does that alignment give you greater confidence in your ability to succeed at what you want to accomplish right now?
>
> ✓ Have you found the intersection between your passion and the marketplace? Do you feel confident you can get paid to do what you enjoy right now? If not, what can you do to get help?

team had been passed over for promotions because of the way they looked."

Lauren completely turned the image, confidence and effectiveness of that team around, so much that she was asked to lead an effort for the entire organization.

"While I was at the bank, I was using my weekends and evenings to do my own thing with the business," she said. "I had incredible productivity levels because I was excited about what I was doing. I had never experienced that kind of energy before."

This was no pipe dream. It was two years of baby steps that took Lauren from "lunch in exchange for a haircut" to the newly created position of vice president of professional image development for her employer. Within six years of that first MBA presentation, she left the bank with a full book of clients in her own consultancy. It took some time but Lauren found the intersection of her passion and the marketplace.

The battle to stay authentic to your call is a never-ending one. Sometimes you might even feel like you've lost sight of that call in the midst of a difficult grad school program or a particularly tough season on the job. You will be confronted with the demons of doubt on a regular basis, but when you find that intersection between your passion and the marketplace, those demons don't stand a chance!

> "Life is not a fairy tale.
> If you lose your shoe at midnight,
> you're drunk."
> — Unknown

SECTION 2
••••
This Ain't No Fairy Tale

DESIGNING YOUR SUCCESS is no fairy tale. We don't click our heels three times and supernaturally get our dream job. There's no Prince Charming coming to save us from our big bad wolf of a boss, and we don't always live happily ever after. Sorry.

This new phase of life is awesome, but it's important now to understand the tradeoffs you'll inevitably have to make if you want to succeed as you turn pro. You're slipping into the driver's seat now (even if you're still in school) and moving forward. It's your responsibility to create the work and life you love. In the midst of doing so, realize this: you won't get everything you want when you want it, your first choice won't always be the right one or best one, and everyone won't always agree with you or support you.

For some of you, your life has been no walk in the park to begin with! You're well familiar with challenge, disappointment, struggle, confusion, self-reliance and lack of support. No one can pull the wool over your eyes with fairy tale fantasies that say "follow your dreams and the money will come!" You know designing your success is going to take commitment in the face of opposition, flexibility and creativity in going after what you want, and a realistic understanding of what the marketplace demands of you.

For others, however, this will be a huge wake-up call.

No matter which perspective you hold right now, this section will impart some of the mental, emotional and professional toughness you'll need to face the unexpected turns in your journey to success.

INSIDER SECRET #6
It Is What it Is

> *"Everything you want in life has a price connected to it."*
> —HARRY BROWNE, writer, politician, investment analyst

A colleague's college-bound son was weighing his career options, and journalism was at the top of his list. She told him candidly, "Journalists don't make a ton of money, but it could be a fascinating life." While there are a few exceptions in the field, such as executive management, national on-air talent, and high-profile columnists, the majority of journalists will generally agree their industry pays awfully, especially in the early years.

Hey, it is what it is.

What often creates discontentment for new grads is that they fail to see people and situations as they are, and then complain that those situations should be different. They don't see their careers as they are. They don't see their workplaces and even their personal relationships as they are, and they don't own the price tag associated with their choices.

Unless you become one of the aforementioned exceptions, becoming a journalist means you won't make a ton of money and that kinda... just... is what it is. That doesn't mean you can't generate money in other ways, such as writing books and freelance articles. Just know the financial rewards might not come right away.

...But it could be a fascinating life.

If you endeavor to be a preeminent figure in your industry and you want to make high six figures in your company and you want to lead people, all of that comes at a price. That price might be getting an advanced degree and working long hours, missing out on happy hours and adventures with your friends, delaying having kids or missing out on time with your family. It might mean challenging co-workers, brutal travel, crazy politics and vacations scheduled around fiscal year-ends, but it is what it is.

If you want greater stability and defined working hours, you might opt for a government career. You will deal with some hair-raising bureaucracy and other experiences that, quite frankly, don't always make a lot of sense.

It is what it is.

If you want greater freedom, flexibility, meaning and control over your own time and money, then you may consider entrepreneurship, and that, too, comes at a price. That price might be a lot of risk, uncertainty, fear and challenges. You might not make money as fast as your college mates who went straight into corporate careers. Entrepreneurship requires putting yourself on a ledge and wondering if you'll emerge as a champ or a chump. It means making money and losing money and figuring out how to make money again. It's never a dull moment and rarely a "safe" one, at least in the beginning.

…but it is what it is.

Many professionals, young and experienced alike, treat their work like a buffet line, where they request the most delectable dishes and discard life's "Brussels sprouts." They want flexible working hours with long-term job security. They want the freedom to come and go as they please, extended vacations and good pay right off the bat.

Sorry, dude, it doesn't work that way. It doesn't work like that on the job. It won't work like that when you get married, and it most definitely doesn't work like that if you ever have kids.

As soon as you recognize what is, and stop fighting what is, you can determine whether you really want what is. I'm all for dreaming big, but there is a measure of realism you must bring to the game when you are making decisions to design your success. Your decisions will become easier because you can honestly embrace the trade-offs associated with your choices—in work, in love, in life—as opposed to denying that trade-offs exist. However, the drawback to acknowledging "what is" becomes that you're now fully accountable for the choices you make. No excuses, no blame-shifting.

It is what it is.

INSIDER SECRET #7
Be Flexible Enough to Change Lanes

"At 22, you think it's all or nothing, in or out, but it doesn't have to be all or nothing. You can back up."
—CHERYL, Washington, D.C., attorney

When I was entering college as an engineering student, a mentor advised me, "Just sacrifice seven years and then it will get better. Seven years and it will be all worth it."

That was the best and absolute worst advice I ever received. It was the best because it equipped me to endure some of the sucky years early in my career, which, in truth, is what we all have to endure on the road to success. But it was the worst because it was incomplete advice and, as a result, I abdicated that inner compass that signaled when I was off-track or when something just didn't feel right. In some instances, that inner compass tells us when we need to make a slight lane shift. Maybe we should do the same job at another company or a different job within the same field. Other times that inner compass is a big, red flashing light signaling us to STOP, back up and high-tail it out of that situation as fast as we possibly can!

I didn't understand any of the signals at the time. I was in that "no-pain, no-gain" career frame of mind, and when it came to discerning right direction for my life, I was deaf, blind and a little slow to get it. The longer I persevered, the better I thought things would be on the other side. After all, my mentor did say give it seven years.

Looking back, I definitely don't regret going the technical route in school because the rigors of the program opened many doors professionally. Moreover, the pain of the process of finding my passions forced me to learn the art of changing lanes, and that skill has saved a lot of tears and added tons of points to the happy column of my life. The best part is that my experience can save you a ton of pain of your own.

A major principle you should understand about designing your success is that, yes, things change. And guess what? You get to change with them! My friend Thomas put it brilliantly when he said:

"For the first 10 years out of college, don't worry about what you're doing. Quit thinking, 'OMG! I gotta get the right career on the right track. Just get on the road.' It doesn't even really matter what direction you're in. There'll be lots of opportunities to change lanes, to turn around and go a different direction. The time for that is not age 21. Ninety-nine percent of 21-year-olds don't know who they are yet. Spend some time figuring out who you are before you worry too much about where you are."

The reality is that where you start in your career may not be where you end. You might graduate in one degree, as I did, then get into the workplace and realize they couldn't pay you enough to do that job! You might set out to medical school convinced pediatrics is for you only to find you simply can't endure the heartbreak when a sick child dies. Or, you might enroll in a culinary program like my friend Courtney, only to find you can't cook under the pressure of a restaurant environment. It will feel like an epic fail in the moment, but when you fast-forward a few years, you will see it's not nearly as big a deal as it seems.

Over the years, I have had a lot of business ideas, and for each venture I would purchase a new domain name in anticipation of my new project. At last count, I had about 16 different website domain names for past and future ventures. You could tell my career direction based on the email domain I was using at the time. I had various real estate ventures, pursued network marketing, conducted women's seminars, you name it. I drove people crazy! As Joey would say, I guess I was following my "passions for now." And through my first, second… fifth try, I uncovered what I believe to be my ultimate life purpose… for now. ☺

In fact, it was those passions for now that revealed some of these insider secrets. My motivations for some of those past pursuits were wildly out of line with who I was and what I wanted. But the good news is I didn't allow ignorance of my ultimate purpose to stop me from moving ahead, and neither should you.

The point here is that things change. You change, and the greatest gift you can give to your future success is to be flexible with how things change. Jasper, an interior designer who started as a research analyst out of college, made an interesting point on this topic.

"I'm not saying you have to travel the world to 'find yourself,' but if you're not certain, you could take a year, reevaluate what you want now that you have your college degree and use the time as an opportunity to explore all those different things you couldn't explore while you were in college.

If you want to do genetic science, great. Find an internship that will allow you to do so in six months. Then you might jump to something else. There's no shame in having two or three internships in a year to just explore what you want. This is the time to do that. It's not as easy as it sounds sometimes, but it's not as hard as it feels either. You might have to get a little creative, take some risks and think outside of the norm to figure it out, but you have more options than just the conventional."

It can be scary to consider changing lanes, especially when so much money, time and energy have been invested in your education, not to mention the expectations of parents and other people you respect. If you have the additional responsibilities of children or family, it can be doubly frightening as you factor family demands into your decisions. Nonetheless, pay attention to the signals that life is sending you to gauge if you are still "right direction" or in need of a shift.

There may be pain associated with making a change, such as extending your graduation by a year, investing in another certification, or taking a step back in pay to gain experience in your new field of interest. But the pain of regret for not doing what you know to be right for you can be far more costly.

INSIDER SECRET #8
Managing "The Others"

"Don't let the noise of others' opinions drown out your own inner voice."
—STEVE JOBS

One of your biggest challenges will be balancing what you believe you want with what others believe is best. It's a big challenge when you're young because you might not be supporting yourself fully on your own, so other people's opinions, like your parents', could have financial implications for you. But the truth is, other people's opinions are a challenge for even the most established professionals. When deciding to leave his director of marketing job, my friend Felix recalled, "I didn't want others to perceive I couldn't hack it. And now I don't know who the 'Others' are. I'm not sure if the 'Others' are my friends, my family or that random person on the street. I don't know, but this nebulous 'Others' ruled over me for a very long time."

I came across a great story to illustrate his point. It's about a man named Monty Roberts, who owns a horse ranch in San Ysidro, Calif. He allows his friend Jack to use the ranch for fundraising events to raise money for at-risk youth programs. One day, he explained to the group of kids why he opens his home:

"I want to tell you why I let Jack use my horse ranch. It all goes back to a story about a young man who was the son of an itinerant horse trainer who would go from stable to stable, race track to race track, farm to farm and ranch to ranch, training horses. As a result, the boy's high school career was continually interrupted. When he was a senior, he was asked to write a paper about what he wanted to be and do when he grew up.

"That night he wrote a seven-page paper describing his goal of someday owning a horse ranch. He wrote about his dream in great detail and he even drew a diagram of a 200-acre ranch, showing the location of all the buildings, the stables and the track. Then he drew a detailed floor plan for a 4,000-square-foot house that would sit on a 200-acre dream ranch.

"He put a great deal of his heart into the project and the next day he handed it in to his teacher. Two days later he received his paper back. On the front page was a large red F with a note that read, 'See me after class.'

"The boy with the dream went to see the teacher after class and asked, 'Why did I receive an F?'

"The teacher said, 'This is an unrealistic dream for a young boy like you. You have no money. You come from an itinerant family. You have no resources. Owning a horse ranch requires a lot of money. You have to buy the land. You have to pay for the original breeding stock and later you'll have to pay large stud fees. There's no way you could ever do it.' Then the teacher added, 'If you will rewrite this paper with a more realistic goal, I will reconsider your grade.'

"The boy went home and thought about it long and hard. He asked his father what he should do. His father said, 'Look, son, you have to make up your own mind on this. However, I think it is a very important decision for you.' Finally, after sitting with it for a week, the boy turned in the same paper, making no changes at all.

"He stated, 'You can keep the F and I'll keep my dream.'"

Monty then turned to the assembled group and said, "I tell you this story because you are sitting in my 4,000-square-foot house in the middle of my 200-acre horse ranch. I still have that school paper framed over the fireplace."

He added, "The best part of the story is that two summers ago, that same school teacher brought 30 kids to camp out on my ranch for a week. When the teacher was leaving, the teacher said, 'Look, Monty, I can tell you this now. When I was your teacher, I was something of a dream stealer. During those years I stole a lot of kids' dreams. Fortunately, you had enough gumption not to give up on yours.'"

> ## *Conversations in the Fast Lane*
> ### *... on This Ain't No Fairy Tale*
>
> ✓ Have you ever felt the need to change directions in some area of your life but were too afraid to do it?
>
> ✓ How have other people's opinions—positive or negative—affected your college or career decisions so far?
>
> ✓ Whether it be with internships, volunteer or professional work, are you taking full responsibility for designing your own success or have you been relying too heavily on others for that?
>
> ✓ Do you feel like you have a pretty realistic view of what the market will demand of you moving forward or have you been a bit naïve?
>
> ✓ What trade-offs do you think you will have to make to pursue a career or business you're interested in right now?

• •

In the quest to design your success, there will be a lot of "Others" weighing in on your life. There's your momma telling you to be safe, your best friend wondering if you're making the right choice, your mentors suggesting the best path forward, and don't forget the split personalities in your head, each with an opinion of its own.

Often, people will not agree with you, and sometimes for very good reasons. Most often, they want the best for you, but sometimes, quite frankly, they don't. You must learn to discern the difference. Other times, people are simply afraid for you. The change you want to make might be in complete opposition to the decision they would make if they were in your shoes. Whatever the reason, respect their viewpoint, evaluate their concerns seriously, and consider ways to overcome or address them.

Believe it or not, there is a gift in every objection, and while people's objections may not affect your decision to change, it might affect how you make the change, thereby increasing your likelihood of success. The bottom line, however, is that no matter how much support or how many voices weigh in, only you are responsible for the consequences of your choices, positively and negatively. Success and happiness starts and ends with you.

"I've come to believe that connecting is one of the most important business (and life) skill sets you'll ever learn."
— Keith Ferrazzi, author and CEO, Ferrazzi Greenlight

SECTION 3
····
Hugs & Handshakes

WHEN IT COMES to your success on the job, relationships are everything. In college, you can secure an internship based largely on your grades and even a less-than-stellar interview performance. You might even eek out your first job knowing nobody but the career center coordinators who managed the on-campus recruiting process.

But don't let that stroke of luck lull you into a false sense of security that you don't have to get out of your comfort zone to initiate and nurture relationships with people at all levels. As Keith Ferrazzi says on the opening page, connecting to people is one of the most important skills you'll ever learn. And he is absolutely, positively, unequivocally right.

When you're young, it's easy to take the people you meet for granted. You assume well-established professionals are way out of your league or too old to relate to your world. You look at your classmates and, for the most part, they're are all broke, a little confused or just trying to figure out life like you are. You have a good time hanging with them, but you never consider how much influence they can have on your future, and that's a classic case of "fast lane, wrong direction."

Believe it or not, some of your friends and classmates are going to come up *big* in life, and you'll wish you had invested in getting to know them when you were all "nobodies." Simple examples from my own life:

• A high school buddy became the global head of learning and development for a large company and hired me for one of my first major corporate contracts as a speaker;

- One of my husband's best friends played in the NBA for several years and is now a broadcaster for pro basketball games all across the country;
- One of my classmates is an Olympic track and field gold medalist. He didn't just compete in the Olympics, he was the best in the world for a moment in time!
- Yet another classmate is an up-and-coming interior designer featured on TV and the hottest design magazines.

When we look back, we all have jacked-up freshman year photos, memories of cramming hard for finals and struggling to navigate through our first jobs. We all have our own fears, insecurities, hopes and dreams. We're all just regular people. But the point is... you never know who those regular people will turn out to be.

Learning to cultivate great relationships over time, whether they be with peers, professors, bosses and people of influence, will be crucial to your success. Doors are opened by *relationships*. Your path is made smoother by *relationships*. One referral call by an acquaintance who is the friend of a hiring manager can be the difference between you getting an interview before a job posts online and the position going to someone else.

How many times have you been banging your head against the wall on a personal or professional problem only to talk with a friend who had the solution—in 10 minutes?! How many times have you been pushed to the next level because one of your friends was living their life at a higher standard? It's the *relationship*.

Hold up, though!

These relationships aren't fostered overnight. You can't just decide to pick up the phone when you need somebody. You must invest along the way, so be very strategic about scheduling these encounters into your life. Your success and the speed with which you attain that success are not solely dependent upon your skill; they are largely dependent on your relationships. There are plenty of not-so-bright people who are doing extraordinary things because of the relationships they keep. Beyond that, successful people who are most balanced and fulfilled are those who have developed rich relationships with which to enjoy the spoils of life.

The bottom line?

It's all about hugs and handshakes, and mastering hugs and handshakes will open more doors for promotion, influence, leadership and opportunity in ways you might never imagine. More than all else, great relationships will expose you to some of the coolest, most enriching experiences ever.

A friend is an attorney in Philadelphia. When I caught up with him, he was running for city council for the second time (he had lost the first campaign). I interviewed him and asked what he would advise the 21-year-old version of himself about success, and he said, "I wish I had spent more time developing networks of friends. I would have pledged a fraternity. I look back and think of the depth of friendship or network of backers I could have now. I didn't take it seriously then."

But *you* are going to take it seriously now. So, let's talk about how hugs and handshakes play out in the real world.

INSIDER SECRET #9
Make Real Friends"

"Networking is rubbish; have friends instead."
—STEVE WINWOOD, musician

When I introduced Hugs & Handshakes, notice I didn't call it by its more commonly known name—networking. That's because when you set out to make real, genuine, helpful connections with people, it's really not "networking" at all. Moving forward, whether you are in the classroom or the boardroom, set out to make friends. I'll talk more in the coming chapters about the specific strategies for doing this, but for now, I simply want you to make the *decision* to do so.

Making real friends is not about manipulating people to see what you can gain from them. It's not about associating with people you don't respect just because it looks good for you to be seen with them. Instead, it's about connecting to people you like, admire and genuinely want in your life. The genuineness with which you approach the most regular of people is the same genuineness with which you can approach the CEO of your company.

In my second job out of college, I was sitting next to the CEO of my company at a small luncheon. Like most, I was tempted to try and impress him with lofty talk about my knowledge of the business, but instead I asked what I thought was the dumbest question ever. I said, "What did you want to be when you were a kid?" He looked taken aback, then pleasantly surprised at the question, and replied, "Right here, right now, leading a company like this, I'm doing exactly what I dreamed of doing when I was a kid." That question opened up a really interesting conversation between the two of us, and an instant connection.

I learned a ton from that exchange. I learned that connecting to people, even "bigger-named" people who might intimate you, is much easier than most of us think. I learned that if I am human first, most people will happily be human in return, even if they are the CEO of the company.

So what does this mean for you? You can't make real friends with other people unless you are…uh…*real*. That means accepting yourself, with all your quirks and idiosyncrasies. Yes, you have areas to change and grow. There are ways you can be better. But in the process of getting better, know now that you are enough. The more you rock *you*, developing a genuine confidence and appreciation for who you really are, the easier and faster you will attract peers, professors and prospective employers to your side. Most professionals take 10 to 20 years to figure out this golden nugget. Master it, and watch the doors of opportunity open up for you in all areas of your life!

INSIDER SECRET #10
Be Interested in Other People

"You can make more friends in two months by becoming interested in other people than you can in two years by trying to get other people interested in you."
—DALE CARNEGIE, writer and lecturer

Reality check: People are not that interested in you. They're not that interested in me. They are interested in themselves–24 hours a day, seven days a week, 52 weeks out of the year. Case in point: You're not reading this book because you're interested in *me*; you're reading it because you're interested in how I can help you get what you want.

If you aim to master Hugs & Handshakes, burn this foundational secret deep in your brain: The most *unproductive* conversation you'll ever have on the job is the one where you do all the talking. You might *feel* good in that conversation because, if we are honest with ourselves, our favorite topic is us—our likes, our dislikes, our wishes, hopes, dreams and goals. If you want to royally bomb a conversation, make it all about yourself. But if you want to make a real, productive connection with someone at any level, focus on them.

When I talk with young professionals on the art of connecting, I encourage them to ask questions that help them to really S.E.E. the other person:

S — Tell me about yourSELF.
- Ask about their family. Where are they from? How long have they been here? What brought them to the area? Do they have kids or siblings?

E — Tell me about your EXPERIENCE.
- Ask about their work. What do they do? Do they like what they do? If so, why? If not, why not? How long have they been at the company? What year are they in their program? What keeps them at their job? What inspires them? What do they hope to do in the future? What are they most proud of in their work? Any big goals for the year?

E — What do you ENJOY?
- Ask about their hobbies and recreation. What did they do over the weekend or spring break? Any trips planned for the summer? What do they enjoy for fun? What do they like about that hobby? Have they won any awards? Do they compete?

The list can go on and on. The point is that when meeting people, the focus of your conversation should be all about the other person. You should really aim to *see* who they are as a person—what excites them, moves them and makes them tick.

Don't just ask these questions; really listen to the answers and be genuinely interested in the individual, even if you're not naturally interested in what they are talking about. Note: To choose to be interested in someone does not mean someone is *interesting*. Being interested in others is a choice of humility and maturity that, quite frankly, most young professionals lack. I encourage you to distinguish yourself by mastering this skill.

I have a 60-year-old client named Jim, who can go on and on about bass fishing. While I will never bass fish a day in my life, I know all about why he likes it and we can talk for ages about it. (Well, *he* can talk for ages. I can ask enough questions to get him to talk for ages!) On the surface, Jim and I have nothing in common and no, I'm honestly not interested in bass fishing. But I am interested in Jim. And Jim becomes interested in me the more interested I am in him. Get it?

When you get interested in other people, you will find things you have in common that you never imagined. You'll quickly connect in ways that can lead to a closer, better, more useful relationship down the road. More importantly, the other person will walk away thinking, "Wow, what a great conversation!" Why? Because it was all about them—*their* likes, *their* dislikes, *their* hopes, dreams and goals.

Keep in mind that people don't always remember what you say or what you do, but they always-always-always remember how you made them feel—good or bad. So, if you want people to get interested in you, get interested in them. Doing so will catapult your career and your life.

INSIDER SECRET #11
What's in It For Them?

"Successful people are always looking for opportunities to help others. Unsuccessful people are always asking, 'What's in it for me?'"
—BRIAN TRACY, author and speaker

Brian Tracy really nails it. The biggest mistake you'll be tempted to make when it comes to networking is the ever-present focus on what's in it for you. That is not what Hugs & Handshakes is all about. The more masterful you get at uncovering what other people need, gifts they would enjoy, introductions that would help, resources that would be valuable—the faster you will make friends who feel an emotional obligation to help you when you need it most. You'll just have to ask, and the answer will be a resounding yes!

I have met a woman named Sarah in passing at a few seminars. We are both speakers, so we remained connected on Facebook and would comment on each other's posts from time to time. One day, I reached out to schedule some time for the two of us to speak. I wanted to learn more about Sarah, her business and how I might be able to help down the road. I had no real agenda; I was just looking for an opportunity to move from being "Facebook friends" to real acquaintances.

We talked for well over an hour, way longer than I had anticipated, and I gave her my thoughts on everything from her branding to her new book. Over time, she would reach out with her new ideas and ask my opinions. Keep in mind, these are "opinions" I actually charge other clients for. When she finally landed on her new brand and logo, she sent me an excited text and thanked me for the role I had played.

Here's where it gets interesting.

Sarah purchased a copy of my book and asked that I send her an autographed copy. When the book arrived, she posted a picture of the cover on her social media page with a very complimentary caption about how excited she was about me and the book. A radio producer in her network saw the post and reached out to me directly, asking if I'd be interested in appearing on a number of radio shows he produced.

Had I reached out directly to that producer to try and get him interested in my work on my own, I would have likely gotten nowhere. But because of Sarah's unsolicited endorsement, I got a ton of free advertising, and this producer's interest was piqued. There is no telling how far the relationship with Sarah or the producer can go in the future—all because I looked for ways to help her—no strings attached.

The above reflects the growing role social media plays in Hugs & Handshakes. You can learn so much about what's happening with people through social media, and through those same channels, you can help them, just like Sarah helped me.

So, instead of merely scrolling your social media feeds to get up on the latest celebrity gossip or funny video, use them as a tool to build relationships. You can congratulate people when you learn of their milestone moments— such as graduation and birthdays—but one strategy to elevate your Hugs & Handshakes is to use social media to promote people you want to connect with.

If someone you know is hosting an event or endorsing a charity, promote that through your network. Tweet about it, share it on Facebook, Twitter, Instagram or whatever your latest platform of choice. If a colleague wrote a book or released an indie album or will be performing at a local comedy club, blast about it on your page. Social media is an easy yet hugely effective way to make an impact on and for people.

Leverage this strategy with everyone you meet—your professors, your bosses, your peers, your mentors. When you support what's important to other people, you build a wicked amount of relationship capital, so keep looking for ways you can serve.

INSIDER SECRET #12
Ask For Nothing

"Don't ask for anything unless it's offered"
—ANDY STOLL, Co-Founder, Seed Here Studio

In the last chapter, you learned how to get interested in other people and find out "what's in it for them." Then what? The important next step is to . . . ask for nothing from people. That's right—ask for absolutely nothing. You're probably wondering, "What's the freakin' point of Hugs & Handshakes if I can't ask for anything?!"

My reply would be, "That's a pretty amateur way to look at Hugs & Handshakes."

You're turning pro now, so you must do this Hugs & Handshake thing like a pro, not like other amateur young professionals who don't have a clue. Now, how do the pros do it? They ask for nothing. Instead, they offer. When you constantly figure out ways that you can serve someone else, in due time (way sooner than you think, actually), people will offer to help you. And when people offer to help you instead of you asking them for help, it's golden.

I met a man, Richard, who exemplified this principle at an event last year. Richard was among many people I met at a three-day conference. We talked about our businesses, cracked a few jokes with one another and exchanged business cards. He said there was someone he thought I should meet. He actually followed up shortly after the conference and made what turned out to be a very quality introduction for me. Richard asked for nothing.

A few weeks later, he did ask me for something, but it wasn't a personal request. He asked me to speak with one of his college mentees who needed some career guidance. Whether I wanted to fulfill his request or not (which I did), the answer was going to be, "Absolutely, yes." Why? Because 1.) I could easily do the favor and 2.) I felt an emotional obligation to do so because he had served me first.

A couple of months later, Richard reached out to me again. No, not to ask for anything. He reached out to serve—again. He learned at the conference where we met that I speak at colleges, so he introduced me as a potential speaker to the assistant director for a group he mentors on a college campus, a perfect contact for me. Had I attempted to get this assistant director interested on my own, it would have been a long shot. But with Richard's reputation and endorsement, she was delighted to consider me for her speaker's lineup.

And still, Richard asked for nothing.

Yet, I am chomping at the bit to find a way to repay the favors. I *want* to offer my support, and when we find the right opportunity to do so, the answer will again be, "Absolutely, yes!"

Now that is how the pros do Hugs & Handshakes.

INSIDER SECRET #13
Don't Keep Score

"My Golden Rule of Networking is simple: Don't keep score."
—HARVEY MACKAY, syndicated columnist

When it comes to Hugs & Handshakes, your only responsibility is to spot *as many opportunities as you can* to add value to someone else's life.

Leverage your own contacts or your parents' contacts to make an introduction for someone. Share a great website or a referral. Alert someone to an event that would be useful to them. Invite someone to an event you're attending that would be of benefit. Or simply remember to check in or follow up with someone if you recall they're going through a hard time or embarking on an important goal. Overwhelm people with genuine, simple, acts of kindness and consideration.

Most of all, however, don't expect anything in return. Don't look for your gesture to be reciprocated. Don't give to receive and don't keep tally on how often you have served someone versus the number of times they've helped you. You miss the point (and the blessings) that come with Hugs & Handshakes if you do that, and you will often find yourself feeling mad, frustrated or cynical of other people.

The reality is the person you are giving to may never give back in the same way, but you will more than receive your payback, now or in the future, in the most unexpected ways. This strategy will make you simply irresistible. Seriously.

INSIDER SECRET #14
Keep in Touch

"Be well, do good work, and keep in touch."
—GARRISON KEILOR, radio personality

This is one of the most overlooked of the insider secrets. People know they should stay in contact, but it's one of those important tasks that most always gets pushed back to "never-ever-happens" land. If you're still in school, this strategy is key because most of your peers don't know to do this. The level of influence and resources you will be able to tap into because you got a head start on keeping in touch will blow your mind. As a young professional, you will see even greater benefits if you actually keep in touch with the people you meet instead of collecting their business cards like you pick up after-dinner mints at a restaurant.

A great online resource to keep in touch with people is LinkedIn. Social media is a fantastic aggregator for your professional and, to some degree, your personal contacts as well. You can keep tabs as people change jobs, launch businesses or have other significant milestones in their career and life.

If you're not on LinkedIn or are not actively using it, change that lickety-split. Take a class on LinkedIn or watch a few videos to learn how that tool works and how to up your game with its resources.

Simple strategies for keeping in touch with people include:

• **Celebrate Them**—Sending a quick congratulations email when someone changes jobs, gets a promotion, gets published, is on TV, has a birthday or some other milestone. Take the extra few minutes to craft a genuine, thoughtful word of encouragement. Banish the one word, "Congrats!" from all future communications, please, and take a few moments to actually say something meaningful;

• **Appreciate Them**—When you accept "friend requests" on social media, take a moment to send a note back thanking them for the invite. Thoughtful people stand out;

• **Consider Them**—When you come across articles, helpful resources or invitations that make you think of someone you know, don't ignore the prompting. Draft a quick email or text and send it to them.

• **Wow Them**—A fun and touching way to reach out to people is with greeting cards. Order a boatload of nice, blank cards on the Internet. When milestones happen, take the time to send a handwritten (yes, *handwritten*) note with your thoughts. As convenient as they are, text messages have zero wow factor—sorry. Most people only get bills in the mail, so trust me, your card will get opened. That means you'll have to be mindful to collect people's business or personal mailing addresses on a regular basis before you need them, but I'm sure you can figure that out.

Keeping in touch is not easy; in fact, it's like a second job. It takes dedication and deliberation with no concern for the immediate payback. But the payback is huge! So make this one of your No. 1 habits. If you don't have the time, make the time. Track your time and find where you are spending any time on "empty calorie activities" such as idle chatter at the water cooler, excessive time on the Internet and email, daydreaming, escaping, or mindless phone or text conversations that add little to no value to your overall growth and happiness. Choose to stop that and replace it by investing your time, however short at the start, in relationships that will progress you.

That is, of course, only if you really intend to maximize your success. Otherwise, skip this secret altogether and move on because knowing what to do without doing what you know is a complete waste of time.

INSIDER SECRET #15
Serve High

"The real currency in networking is generosity, not greed."
—KEITH FERRAZZI, author

Contrary to pop culture, real impact is not about having the world look at you and be impressed with your achievements, your status or your looks. Real impact is about leveraging your achievements, status, looks, etc. to contribute to the world in ways that make people's lives better.

"Better" can manifest itself from technological innovations and social justice to philanthropy and yummy food. When you leverage your achievements, status, looks, etc. for good, you invariably attract more achievements, more status and yes, guys, you can even appear better-looking!

So what does this mean for you? As you master Hugs and Handshakes, look to broaden your relationship impact in three ways: by serving high, reaching across and lifting up. I'll cover serving high here, then address the other two ways to broaden your impact in subsequent chapters.

With Serve High, we all have people that we look up to yet feel are so far out of our league. They may be senior executives, mentors, gurus, icons or simply wildly successful people who intimidate us. One endorsement from them, if they like or believe in us, could open the door to an internship, fellowship or dream-come-true opportunity.

Your goal is not to get "in" with these people or even try to impress them, as most short-sighted young professionals try to do. Your goal is to serve them, support them and advance their causes. No, you might not be able to make a meaningful business introduction for them yet. But, you can volunteer for one of their events. You can donate a few bucks to an important cause they are supporting. You can promote their products, services, events and lectures. You can be an evangelist to build their brand, profile or business.

The prideful part of you might resist and say, "Please, I'm nobody's groupie, and I'm no suck-up." What I am sharing is not about kissing butt. It is about advancing the lives of people you admire and believe in the same way you would want that person to do for you (if they had a clue who you were!). You might recognize this strategy as "The Golden Rule"–you know–do unto others as you would have them do unto you. If you want to get super philosophical, I can reference the what-goes-around-comes-around, reaping-and-sowing karma kick, but I trust you get the message.

What's wild is that hardly anybody does this, but my friend Stacey Martino does. We follow similar teachers for our life and business, and we've done a lot of work with Tony Robbins, a world-renowned peak performance coach and motivational speaker. Stacey is the kind of person who will shout from the rooftops if she finds a service provider who does great work, and Tony Robbins is legendary, Stacey and I agree.

But she is the one who would post links to Tony's live seminars when they come to town. She would wholeheartedly endorse him and share public reviews on how his work improved her marriage and influenced how *she* became the founder of RelationshipDevelopment.org.

Stacey wasn't good friends with Tony Robbins or anything like that. She was one of the millions of people who had attended his seminar, just like me. But Stacey believed in his value and elevated him without any ulterior motive. So, when Tony Robbins launched another TV campaign on QVC to sell his products, who was invited to Skype on national TV to talk about her personal results? And when Stacey got certified as a relationship coach through Tony Robbins' organization and launched her own products and seminars, guess whose website was featured on the Robbins' webpage and in the email blast that went out to millions of people worldwide?

Let's just say it wasn't Renessa Boley Layne; it was Stacey Martino!

Stacey simply served high. She invested in someone she admired, whose work she believed in, and she used whatever sphere of influence she had to advance his business. Those simple gestures came back to bless her, big time.

INSIDER SECRET #16
Reach Across

"Help other people achieve their dreams and you will achieve yours."
—LES BROWN, motivational speaker

The second group of people to focus on as you expand your network are your peers–your fellow students, interns, young professionals who, like you, are trying to move and shake their own lives.

What's funny is of the three groups, this one might actually be the hardest for you to network because, although you may respect your peers for their accomplishments, at times you may also feel competitive, insecure or even jealous. There's often a fear that if you show vulnerability to your peers, they might discover you're the fraud you fear yourself to be.

What will they think if you fail on the job, if you can't hack it with this big idea you call a business? What if they succeed faster than you? What if you fall behind? What if they one-up you?

When it comes to our peers, we often fall into a trap of comparing ourselves to them, and as a result, we are often reluctant to help them. But as counterintuitive as Les Brown's quote above might seem, it could not be truer. The more you help your peers reach their goals, the more you'll reach your own.

Obviously, you should exercise wisdom to ensure people don't take advantage of you, but the truth is that at some point, someone will. Notice Les Brown's quote did not say, "Help others achieve their dreams and [they will help] you achieve yours." *They* might not do a daggone thing in return and, in those moments, it might sting

> ## *Conversations in the Fast Lane*
> ### *... on Hugs & Handshakes*
>
> Often we don't value relationships until we need them, and we're embarrassed in those moments to realize how few deposits we have made into relationships when it's time to make a withdrawal. So, below are three specific strategies you can use to generate more hugs and handshakes to not only boost your career, but increase the passion, adventure and excitement with which you live your life:
>
> ✓ **You Pay**—Even if you are an intern or new college grad with limited funds, set aside money from your paycheck to invite a co-worker to lunch. It doesn't have to be an expensive meal; you could spend less than $10 at the on-site cafeteria in your building or at one of the local food trucks. If you're really broke, it could be as simple as a coffee or smoothie, so don't complicate the idea. The gesture, however, will go a long way with people because it is so unexpected from someone your age. Usually, it's the more experienced professional who feels the pressure to treat. These random acts of kindness are priceless and people will remember you for them;
>
> ✓ **Schedule "Value Networking"**—Set aside time on your calendar once a quarter (every three months) to think of ways you can help people in your network. Do they need a business referral or help with an event they are hosting? Do they need you to spread the word about something or donate to their fundraiser? That's what people will remember you for—support of what's important to *them*.
>
> ✓ **Go "Old School"**—Email, text and other forms of technology are far less personal and endearing. When opportunity presents, send a hand-written note, a real birthday or congratulations card, an actual (inexpensive) gift. Yes, it will take more time and thought, but you will stand out!

something fierce. Nevertheless, when there is an opportunity to make an introduction for someone else, support their cause or event, or help them to become better in their work, *do it!*

They might not reciprocate in kind, but that doesn't matter. Someone else will come to your benefit. It's one of those secrets to success that simply works.

INSIDER SECRET #17
Lift Others Up

"We rise by lifting others."
—ROBERT INGERSOLL, Civil War veteran, political leader

This is one of those short, sweet and to the point secrets. Whatever gift you have—whether you are a tech whiz, a budding fashion designer, an athletic phenom or a literary genius—it has been given to you for the purpose of making someone else's life better. Don't lose sight of that.

I believe you should be generously compensated for the skills and value you bring to world. Make all the money you are due. But remember to say "yes!" to opportunities for being charitable with your gifts without need or thought to the compensation. I am not suggesting you go into debt to serve, but be on the lookout for ways you can build your network *through* service. What skill do you have that you can donate for free?

You'll certainly benefit from the warm and fuzzies that come with helping people in need, and that's blessing enough on its own, but other people will also see your talent on display. You never know the quality of people you will connect with and the referrals they can make on your behalf when you are in service *together* to something greater than your own advancement.

You'll recognize soon enough that sometimes "free" pays back dividends you never imagined.

> "The single-most powerful asset is our mind.
> If trained well, it can create enormous wealth."
> — Robert Kiyosaki

SECTION 4
· · · ·
Your Competitive Advantage

MUCH LIKE YOUR abs are at the core of your ability to sculpt a rockin' body, your mindset is your competitive advantage in the world of work. Whatever big dreams you have for yourself is going to require things most people are not willing to do. The reason I have dedicated an entire section to your mindset is because advancing in your career and in life doesn't start with what you do. It doesn't start with your talents. It doesn't even start with your network.

It starts with how you *think*.

Believe it or not, all of our fears (the non life-threatening ones, anyway) boil down to two simple root questions:

1.) Will I be loved?

2.) Am I enough?

If you trace every fear you've had of doing most anything, whether it was talking to a beautiful girl on campus, pledging to a sorority or fraternity, or going on your first job interview, the fear was likely rooted in one of those two questions. If you try to explain every crazy, destructive or counterproductive behavior you've ever displayed, it, too, would be rooted in one or both of those questions.

The irony is that the answer to those questions is always a resounding *yes*! That doesn't mean you're always right (just ask your parents!), nor does it mean you'll be good at everything you try (Google *American Idol's* William Hung.). It also doesn't mean everyone will applaud you, but that doesn't make the statement any less true. You are loved—always. And you are enough—always, regardless of whether anyone ever agrees with you.

Before you start dismissing this as "woo-woo" psychobabble, consider how profound and truthful this realization is for a lot of young professionals. Most of us have never been taught to view ourselves as innately worthy; instead, we've been taught to seek *validation*. There is a difference. Our value and achievements are disproportionately influenced by how other people view us. We seek validation from our professors, parents, friends, boyfriends and bosses. We desire someone to praise and validate our job as well done. We make a funny comment on social media, and we're disappointed if it doesn't get as many LOLs or retweets as we expected. Our need for validation influences nearly every aspect of our lives.

A hugely successful real estate investor told me something that really hit home: "Put us in the spotlight for a moment and we'll perform, but sit us down by ourselves and ask us if we really believe we're as good as they say we are, and we're in trouble."

If someone were to ask if you are confident, you would likely say, "Yes." Even if you didn't actually believe it, you would assume the person asking expected you to be confident, so you would be an idiot to say, "No." But I challenge you on why you believe you are confident, if you indeed do. Are you confident because of what you have done and what you have accomplished in school or on the sports field, or are you confident because of who you *are*?

I was confronted with the answer to that question in a big way in my 20s when I started investing in real estate. It was my first go at financial freedom and I started investing in houses left and right with a former roommate and business partner. It was a successful run in many respects and a total debacle in others.

The relationship started out exciting and over time disintegrated into the partnership from hell! I should have ended the partnership two years before it actually fell apart. I was unhappy, felt disrespected and came to really resent my partner. But at my core I felt I couldn't accomplish the big dreams I had for the business without her, so I endured a really bad dynamic to keep those dreams alive.

I was the primary financier for the business, which meant I had the money. I certainly brought other skills to the table, but I was a grasshopper in my own eyes. She was more assertive, more aggressive and quick on her feet. In hindsight, I realize that some of her qualities weren't necessarily the most endearing. She could be domineering, but at the time I thought I needed her partnership to be successful. She was definitely a very talented person and an asset to the team. I'm a firm believer that when choosing to partner with someone, they should bring skills to the table that you lack. Otherwise, why partner?

But you never *need* anyone at the expense of your own happiness and self-respect, and that's where I tripped. We had a fair business partnership for the most part, but the interpersonal dynamic sucked because I didn't have confidence in my own value. As a result, I allowed her to run over me emotionally. I was too insecure to take a stand for how I should have been treated. I thought I was enduring the discomfort and resentment for the sake of the business when, in actuality, it was because I didn't believe I was good enough to succeed without her.

When you are driven by ego, whether in the form of insecurity as I was or a need for external validation, you can be manipulated to do anything. I reflect on that time of my life and think, "What the [bleep]?!" I would have never thought in a million years that I—a high school valedictorian, Stanford University grad, six-figure earner—would have allowed someone to treat me that way, but because I couldn't fully appreciate my own value at the time, I did.

Here's what I know for fact: You will fail, you'll screw up royally, and while you can't possibly realize it now, some of your biggest failures will be the seed to your greatest successes. When you do lose, you must deeply ingrain it in your head that you are always-always-*always* worthy of another shot, a second chance, another swing at bat. You're even worthy enough to walk away if you find a situation, circumstance or even a relationship no longer serves your highest good.

If you don't truly know your value in those dark moments, you might pick yourself up using some pretty destructive means, such as drugs, alcohol, sex, cheating, emotional and physical disorders. Worse, you might not have the courage to pick yourself up at all. If you don't know your own worth, it will be nearly impossible to follow your dreams. Realizing your full potential for success, as well as the ability to actually *feel* successful, may hinge on mastering this insider secret.

INSIDER SECRET #18
The Fraud Syndrome

*"I have written eleven books, but each time I think,
'Uh oh, they're going to find out now. I've run a game on everybody,
and they're going to find me out.'"*
—MAYA ANGELOU, author, poet, civil rights activist

You would be amazed how prevalent low self-esteem is among achievers. It doesn't matter if you were bounced around the foster care system as a child or came from a two-parent home with a white picket fence, your self-worth (or lack thereof), could be impacting you in ways you never imagined.

Low self-esteem takes on many forms that aren't usually obvious to the people around you. Ironically, some people mask a lack of confidence by achieving even more, but no amount of achievement will satisfy you until you realize the value of who you are.

If your self-worth in the past has been tied to the level of your achievement, you may likely be experiencing what I call the "Fraud Syndrome." The "Fraud Syndrome" is the idea that you're never quite good enough, and at any moment, someone is going to discover you don't deserve all those kudos, you're really a mess inside, and you're barely keeping it together. As with Maya Angelou in the opening quote, somebody is going to find out you're a fake.

One of my coaching clients, a lawyer, described it perfectly when she shared her reaction to starting at her first law firm:

"The desire to be special and different was exacerbated at the firm. When I became a regular fish surrounded by so many other smart people, I felt like a phony. I really didn't belong and eventually they would find out."

Wow. This woman completed Yale undergrad and Georgetown Law School. By all external accounts, she was hot stuff. When we met, she was working for one of the premier law firms in the country, yet she didn't feel as if she belonged. We worked together as she transitioned out of law to start her own real estate investment company, something she is tremendously passionate about. She confessed to me some time later:

"Maybe I should have stayed to make partner just to prove I could. There's something in me that feels bad for not being the best. Then there's a part of me that says, 'Yeah, you should have left because you weren't really good enough.'"

That is the classic case of the "Fraud Syndrome." I have experienced it many times before and with so many people, young and old, that I have coached. No matter how good you are, in your own mind you're never good enough, and that's assuming all is well in your world. When all is not well and you are in a season of failure or disappointment, all hell often breaks loose in your mind. In those moments, the anxiety, fear and insecurity can be unbearable no matter how put-together you look to your friends.

When we are in the grip of the "Fraud Syndrome," we mask it in many ways, but the symptoms of self-worth deficiency are unmistakable. Here are some common and fairly obvious coping signs:

- **Food Is King**—If you find yourself pigging out or snacking insessantly when you feel stressed or insecure, that might be an indication of self-esteem issues;
- **The Party Rules**—Your life is all about partying, clubbing and hitting all the right spots, and you find it hard to be still, be quiet or be alone;
- **Excessive Status Indicators**—You have a checklist and need to hang in "this" circle, or be in-the-know with "this" group of people;
- **You Pride Yourself on the "Chase"**—If you're churning through women (or men) without true gratification, it's time to check yourself (and your ego) ;
- **You Use Drugs and Alcohol as an Escape**—You don't have to be a full-blown alcoholic to have an issue here. If you find yourself plopped on the couch escaping with a glass of wine or beer most nights, it's time to question;
- **You're Bartering For Love**—Otherwise known as people pleasing, bartering for love is a little deceptive because your motives can appear to be so much about other people when, in actuality, they're all about you. You may find yourself giving to people or doing things to win friendship, love, acceptance and approval. With this motive, you will often feel disappointed, wondering why the very thing you want continues to elude you. You must value yourself before anyone else's validation will satisfy you.

I've dedicated two chapters to closely related topics about esteem and worth, but it's crucial that you get the point of these insider secrets. In all your achieving, in your ambitions for grad school, starting a business or the next promotion, invest time and energy to build your intellectual, emotional and spiritual muscles to be confident in who you are, *not* just what you achieve. It's easier said than done, for sure, so don't be surprised that you can't simply willpower the negative thoughts away.

In my 20s, I spent a fair amount of money investing in my personal growth because I had been conditioned for years to not value myself in the right ways. This kind of focus on mental and emotional resilience was not common for a person my age, but I quickly learned from mentors that my happiness and success depended on me having a deeper confidence in myself, a confidence that went below the surface.

While it was never their intention, my parents conditioned me at a very early age to align my self-worth to my achievements. One of my parents had never graduated high school, so they wanted far more for me and pushed me to get it. As a result, "second place was first loser" in my world, so if I wasn't the best, if I wasn't number one, I wasn't good enough. The problem with that mindset is that there is a cycle to success. Every time I mastered one stage of life, I'd rise to the top and get elevated to the next level. Then guess what happened? I'd end up at the bottom of that new level—learning, growing, practicing, trying—until I mastered the skills required to elevate again.

During that neverending cycle, sometimes I would blow it out (a good thing), sometimes I would stink it out (not so good). Sometimes I was the best in the room; other times I was lucky just to be in the room. That's the normal ebb and flow required to eventually be a badass in your work, but I didn't understand that at the time. My fear of not always measuring up certainly fueled me to work harder, but it also caused me to avoid taking risks that could have led to some really cool opportunities.

Your personal battle with the fraud syndrome might not stem from well-intentioned parents with a flawed achievement philosophy. Yours could be rooted in physical or sexual abuse as a child, trauma, abandonment, instability, poverty, psychological issues or a whole host of other reasons. That does not mean you need therapy, necessarily, but it does mean that you must be very deliberate about building up your self-esteem. It is so easy to focus on your performance at work, your technical skills, networking or creating a business plan than to deal with the real key to your success—your mindset and your emotions.

You will gain a massive competitive edge in the marketplace when you learn to manage your self-esteem, but success in this area is not a do-it-yourself activity; you don't have to go it alone. If this chapter resonates with you, invest in books or audios that speak to your specific self-esteem issues, attend personal growth seminars, hire personal coaches or therapists, leverage your mentors as sounding boards and surround yourself with people who reinforce your awesomeness.

I am giving you a behind-the-curtain peek into the minds of many people you look up to, but who would be too embarrassed to reveal this secret to you. It takes most people decades to get comfortable with truly understanding their worth and separating their worth from their achievements. As a result, they experience years of secret pain and frustration while looking awesome to the outside world. That doesn't have to be you. You deserve more than looking the part of success; you deserve to truly be it. So if that means going to a few less movies or happy hours with friends so that you have the money to invest in mindset activities that will advance you in your career and life, do it. Mastering this insider secret is non-negotiable.

INSIDER SECRET #19
Kid Stuff

"Inside every older person is a younger person wondering what the hell happened!"

—UNKNOWN

When you were a kid, life was pretty simple. Whether you grew up poor and struggling or with a silver spoon in your mouth, how you viewed life was pretty straightforward. When it came to friends, you either liked them or you didn't. When it came to food, you either wanted it or you didn't. When it came to playtime or chores or anything else, you either loved it or you hated it.

Simple.

But you may have already noticed that as you get older, life gets more complicated, or at least it feels that way. And that's how we end up "wrong direction" in our career, school, business, even our love life, and have no idea how to fix it.

That's why insider secret #21 is to never lose sight of the kid in you. The kid in you owns what you're passionate about without apology. The kid in you almost always knows what it wants, even if he doesn't know exactly how to get it. The kid in you doesn't trade what it truly wants for what you think your mom wants for you or what your professor says you should want. The kid knows that, when it comes to career, if it ain't fun, it's not the line of work for you, no matter how much money you can make.

So, find the little kid you thought you had to leave behind when you officially became an "adult." Consult with that kid every now and then and pay attention to the words of wisdom from that inner guide who has no ulterior motive other than to make you happy. Make time to play, laugh, create, and try new things despite your fears. Jump out of trees, metaphorically. Little boys and girls jump out of trees all the time and, yes, sometimes they break an arm or a leg. But they turn those casts into "body art" until they're well enough to climb another tree!

Like the kid in you, you might have to eat life's Brussels sprouts, not because they taste good, but because they're good for you. You might have go through the discomfort of learning something new or you might have to work like mad for a degree or a promotion, but those are just life's Brussels sprouts. You may have to eat life's Brussels sprouts every now and again, but that doesn't mean you have to skip dessert!

INSIDER SECRET #20
Be Persistent

"For success, don't take the path of least resistance. Take the path of most persistence."
—MICHELE JENNAE, founder, Artuitive Academy

Michele Jennae's opening quote is spot on when it comes to experiencing "fast lane, right direction." There is absolutely no better time to integrate these success secrets into your life than right now. I'll talk more about *why* there is no better time in the section, "Milk Your Age For All It's Worth," but for now, I ask you to simply accept this as true.

So how can you use this ripe window of opportunity to your advantage? You've got to invest and be persistent. An athlete at the top of their game has to be diligent, dedicated and persistent in practice, on the field and in how they take care of themselves off the field. If you are top of your game academically, think about how much time and energy you invested beyond the basics required of you to excel. Same goes for excelling musically or in a business you may have started. You must take the strategies you're learning in this book and *be persistent* in applying them.

Sometimes you will see the fruit of these strategies right away and sometimes it will take a while. The secret is that the delay is not a sign the strategies aren't working. The delay is a test. If things have come easily for you up until this point—e.g., you've had parents, teachers or coaches to open doors for you—it's about to get rough. Why? Because you're embarking on the testing phase; life is about to see what you're really made of. You may experience challenges with your co-workers or have conflict with your boss. You may start to question whether you're in the right job or experience personal issues that impact your work. Remember these are just tests, checkpoints on the road to develop you into the person you need to be to succeed in the fast lane.

In high school we used to chant this cheer: "You've got to want it to win it and we want it more!" Your level of persistence in making real friends, in keeping in touch with people, and applying other strategies from the book will reveal if you indeed want it more.

INSIDER SECRET #21
Stay in Your Own Lane

> *"There's no need to ever compare yourself to someone else.*
> *The world is waiting for 'you.'*
> *Nobody, I mean nobody, does that better than you."*
> —RENESSA BOLEY LANE, author, *Fast Lane, Wrong Direction*

Have you ever found yourself fired up about the latest happenings in your life? Maybe you lost 10 pounds, got the fellowship you'd been competing for or bought your first new car.

Whatever it was, life was looking up!

That is... until you ran into your "Biggest Loser" friend who shed 25 pounds to your 10, or the dude who got into the MBA program you were rejected from, or the friend who just clocked a signing bonus and stock options for their new role while you're barely making ends meet on your "dream job." There is no faster way to douse cold water on our accomplishments than by comparing where we are to where someone else is, and I can't think of any flaw more pervasive in the fast lane makeup than the obsession with comparisons.

Let's be real: Competition is an essential part of life. There can only be one Super Bowl-winning team each year, one president of the United States, one Miss America pageant queen. But when it comes to the game of success, as preschoolish as it may sound, everybody can be a winner.

The rules to the game are different and, consequently, the rules for experiencing fast lane, *right direction* are hinged on our ability to free ourselves from the negative impact of comparing our progress with that of other people.

I'm embarrassed to admit this, but I was watching an episode of "American Idol" one night, and something got me to thinking about Ryan Seacrest and how rich he must be, given the reality show, radio show and all the other things he's doing. Then I thought, "I wonder how old he is?" Everything in me hoped he was in his mid-40s, because somehow that would make me feel better about myself, as if I still had time to reach the level of my own ambitions. So, of course, I went to the all-knowing source of information (Google) and discovered, to my dismay, that he was only a few months older than me.

Are you freakin' kidding me?!?!

Then I began to compare our timelines: When did he start broadcasting? When did he land his first commercial gig? When did this start, when did that start? It turns out Seacrest practically had a microphone in his hand before he could walk, and throughout his entire life he took steps that moved him in the direction of his passion. My dismay had nothing to do with his riches; I envied his ability to F.O.C.U.S (Follow One Course Until Successful). When we look at his professional life, at least, we see the fruit of that focus and the years of seasoning and experience that have culminated into his current success.

Why couldn't it have happened that way for me?
Why did I have to flail about for over a decade trying to discover my purpose?
Why was my life marked by a dead-end pursuit of unfulfilling ambitions?

I would have "focused" and paid my dues if only I had a focus. *Why not me?* I could feel the engine of comparison revving up and I knew that would only put me in the "my life sucks" state, which is always unproductive, right? Instead, I chose to get inspired by the possibilities of what a focused life could produce and recognize that we each have a purpose for our lives, and that purpose is fulfilled through great highs and great lows. No one escapes either end of the spectrum.

All we see with Ryan Seacrest is the flash. We don't know what people went through to get what they got, how they might suffer to keep it or who they are behind closed doors. So often, when we are "boo-hooing" about why we aren't where someone else is, we have failed to read to the end of our own story.

I can't imagine doing anything else with my life than what I am currently doing, and I know that purpose was revealed through the frustration and confusion of the prior years. When I coach my clients, I can literally articulate their pain in ways that blow them away. I can anticipate their next moves, what they're thinking, what their insecurities are without them saying a word. I can ask that profound question when I speak in front of an audience that will cut right to the heart of everything they're trying to avoid.

Why? Because I have been there. And in the same way that I couldn't possibly do what Ryan Seacrest does the way he does it, nobody can do me better than me.

My friend Joey is owner of a branding firm in Denver. He shares how comparisons affected him in the early stages of his business:

"I was bumping into law school buddies out and about in Washington D.C., and, of course they're all saying, 'I'm on the partner track at whatever law firm,' and here I was starting my own business—no health insurance, working out of my apartment, eating peanut butter and jelly sandwiches, doing everything to fund the business. It didn't take me too long to recognize I was happier than they were. When that really started to sink in, it helped me justify what I was doing. It was a few years afterward when I became fully comfortable with the fact that I had walked away from the lucrative power attorney career to start my own business and really do what I like to think of as lifestyle design—creating and shaping the kind of life I wanted instead of the kind of life others expected."

Who hasn't had one of those situations where you wish you could crawl into a hole at the sight of somebody you envy? Often it's not the "I-wish-you-were-dead" kind of envy, but more of the "I suck" kind of envy. Joey's story is not about bashing attorneys; there are plenty of lawyers who thrive in their roles and you might be well on your way to law school, studying for the bar, or getting your first crack at practicing. Instead, this is about gaining clarity for what you want in your career and staying in your own lane, independent of what your peers appear to be doing.

If you miss this secret, you will never enjoy whatever success you currently have, whether it's leading your first project team at work or publishing your first article in a major paper. You will find yourself chasing a moving target because there will always be someone who gets promoted faster, has a hotter girlfriend or a better body. You might one-up the next person here or there, but the comparison game is one you ultimately cannot win.

When you deliberately rid yourself of competition in the game of life and recognize that your success, happiness and worth are never relative to someone else's, you will succeed—and *enjoy* it. Removing that competition is one of the hardest qualities to master because it takes guts, courage, heart, strength, balls and any other synonym you can think of to finally achieve. But if you choose to stay in your own lane, you will become world-class more effortlessly and your happiness will no longer be at the whim of the next man's ego trip.

INSIDER SECRET #22
Character Matters

"Character is the real foundation of all worthwhile success."
—JOHN HAYS HAMMOND, mining engineer and philanthropist

Senior managers and established entrepreneurs often talk about the next generation of leaders. What's often at the top of that conversation is not a young person's skill, but their character. It's the evaluation of how they show up in the marketplace, who they are as a person, and whether they represent the best of what's good in the world. Skill matters but character is your "secret sauce."

That's why Hammond's opening quote has so much validity. On one hand, character is invisible, yet on the other it's the most noticeable thing about you. When I encounter young college grads, I can quickly detect a person of good character and one who is lacking. For instance, do they honor our appointments or do they blow off my time, showing up late or canceling at the last-minute. Do they value my advice as a more established professional or do they present themselves as a know-it-all in conversation?

A colleague, John, once asked me to have a conversation with one of his mentees, a college senior named Ava. She was feeling overwhelmed about her post-grad career path and didn't know what to do. In her initial email to me, she wrote:

> I've struggled to figure out how to go down the right career path when I don't necessarily know exactly what it is I would like to do. Public relations has been something I've been thinking about a lot, but I would also love to pursue my dream of screenwriting as I'm working toward that at the Second City. But I was hoping we could discuss 1.)

How you would suggest being productive without knowing a direct path; 2.) Do you have any advice for someone young and ambitious like myself, but feels conflicted in what direction to go? And 3.), how did you find your path? Thank you very much for your time. I am usually available all day on Tuesdays and Thursdays.

There was a lot baked in her questions, but no problem—it was right up my alley—and as a favor to John, I was more than happy to help Ava in any way I could. So I reached out to offer a time to meet on one of the days *she* indicated she was available. She replied that she was now unavailable. I offered another option the next week; she wasn't available then either. In fact, this is how Ava replied:

Hi Renessa,

I actually have an interview Tuesday morning and I am busy Thursday morning as well unfortunately. And after this week, I start the spring semester and my availability will change again. Would you just like to email?

Best,

Ava

My first thought was, "Umm…I'm sorry. Who's asking for the help here? You or me?" My second thought was, "There's no way in hell I'm having a whole discourse around all your life questions via email! I don't have time for that."

Ava's response reflected a lack of maturity and character, something we've all had to develop at some point. That, coupled with the fact that I was doing a favor for John left me *still* open to meet with her. But I gave John a rundown on the exchange so that he could "help her out."

Here was John's response:

Renessa,

I appreciate your email on so many facets!! Most people wouldn't have been as flexible as you have to meet with her. And most certainly, almost nobody anymore takes the time to close the loop, yet alone write a detailed reply. I have been working with her on the importance of being flexible, being appreciative, being respectful, and being prepared. The fact that she missed on all fronts, and I have your words, not mine, to reinforce the lesson will be impactful. So I absolutely will be using this as an "effective teaching point." That's amazing that you are still open to connecting, and if SHE chooses to step up her game, perhaps you will hear from her.

Ava never chose to "step up her game" and fix this.

It goes back to character.

Character would have valued the advice and time I was willing to dedicate to her. Character would have shown greater humility, urgency and flexibility—the very qualities Ava and her mentor had been discussing—to make the call happen around my schedule, not hers. After all, she was asking for *my* help, and the one in need *needs* to be most flexible, always. Once John pinpointed the error, character would have reached out to me to make it right, Character would have done one or all of those things; Ava did none of them.

The point here is that people will talk about how you show up in the market, how you value their time, how you respect their expertise. They may never tell you, but little things like that influence people's perceptions of you in big ways. Ava left such a first impression on me that she became the poster child in this book for what *not* to do when building relationships with people who can help you!

If you're looking to develop strong character, trust me, you won't have to search too hard for opportunities. Life will give you plenty of chances, usually presented as really uncomfortable and often unpleasant tests, to build your character muscles! The question is whether you will recognize and pass the tests when they show up.

What kind of tests should you expect? Well, I'm glad you asked!

Character tests will come in various forms and from all directions—on the job, within your closest relationships, through the pursuit of your big dream. They will commonly challenge the following aspects of who you are:

• **Ethics**—Are you committed to doing what's right by your company, your clients and your peers, even when opportunities to do wrong present greater gain for your success?

• **Integrity**—To what extent are you committed to being honest and upright personally and professionally? Do you do what you say you are going to do, fulfill your commitments, meet your deadlines? These are all elements of integrity;

• **Courage**—Inevitably, we all must put on our big boy pants. This may mean initiating a workplace conversation you'd rather avoid, going against the grain of your team or advocating for yourself in pursuit of something you want. Whether you stand up or shrink back in those moments will be a test of your character;

• **Honor**—Many of us like to be honored but most don't *give* honor. Extending respect, esteem, appreciation and value for other people regardless of whether they are above or below you on the professional totem pole is the true essence of honor;

• **Humility**—Often, our egos usually can't stomach the spirit of generosity required to genuinely praise other people. I mean, if you honor and promote your peer, *they* might get the promotion, *they* might look better before the boss, *they* might climb the ladder faster, right?

Wrong! Oh so wrong! If you can exalt others, you will inevitably be exalted, be it by promotion, recognition or unexpected opportunities that turn out for your benefit. My experience shows, however, that you may have to fail this test a few times before you develop the humility to pass it. But when you do, the world will open up for you!

• **Reliability**—Do you do what you say you're gonna do when you say you're gonna do it, and do you do it with *excellence*. News flash: Just because you did something doesn't mean you did it to the best of your ability. Half-stepping, whether with your personal or professional commitments, is a sure-fire way to fail the reliability test;

• **Responsibility**—Take responsibility for what you are responsible for when things go well and especially when things go poorly. No excuses, no blame-shifting, no lies;

• **Resilience and Perseverance**—How well do you bounce back after a setback? How long do you sit in a corner and lick your wounds after you fail? Will you try one more time to get it right or will you give up because it feels so hard. There's a hefty price to pay for success and part of that price is measured by your ability to just stick with it when things are rough.

Can you skip class on the days that character is taught? Sure you can, and for a while it may seem like no big deal. You might experience quick monetary success, but let's be real. . . that happens all the time, for the noble and the jerks alike. What most young professionals don't realize is that you will always be brought down to the level of your personal and spiritual growth—your *character*. You will make the money and somehow lose it. You will be elevated, then demoted. There are countless examples of that in business, ministry, sports and pop culture.

Young people believe they will be the exception. It's not true. You can't fake mastery, integrity and authenticity. At least, not for long. You will eventually be uncovered and you'll pay the price, publicly or privately. Why? Because character matters.

INSIDER SECRET #23
The Need For Speed

"We've grown up in a society where everything needs to happen right now... I felt like a failure because my product came out late. But the truth is, there is always someone who is going to need what I do."

—ABIGAIL, entrepeneur

One of the awesome qualities about fast-laners is we get stuff done—*fast!* The Achilles' heel of fast-laners, however, is we get stuff done fast — complete with Band-Aids, duct tape, twisty ties and pantyhose to hold it all together. We will break our necks to meet some imaginary window for success, largely based on some record a guru or mentor set as an example. It goes something like this:

"If so and so earned their first six-figure check in two years, then that's what I'm going to do! I don't need to eat, sleep or shower (okay, maybe shower). The friends can wait, I don't have time to date, momma knows I love her, but I'm on a mission... to lead the project, to make partner, to pass the Bar, to win the gold medal. And I need to do it now-now-now-now-now! I'm late. I'm behind. I need to catch up. Let's go!"

When marketing their expertise to you, gurus often fail to mention it took them eight years of trial, error and investment to learn the skills that equipped them to sell that million-dollar app in two years. They fail to share that they would give up half their earnings to get back what they sacrificed in exchange for speed.

Minor marketing oversight, right? Wrong.

In the meantime, we are wearing ourselves out, we're unhappy, we can't celebrate, and when we finally get "there" (wherever there is!), it's not nearly as satisfying as we thought it would be. Worse, we can't remember any of the joys of the journey along the way.

Your need for speed has various roots. You might be broke and eager to no longer be broke, so the faster you make money, the faster you are no longer broke. I've been there. For others, it's rooted in ego; you want to be the youngest X or the fastest

Y. Still, for others, it's rooted in this internal sense of failure. If you don't accomplish something in the same time frame as someone else, then somehow you're not as good as they are.

Whatever the reason, the need for speed at the expense of mastery, depth and quality or for the satisfaction of ego rarely has lasting power and always creates a tremendous amount of insecurity and discontentment. We can all agree that every great success story starts with a small beginning. Apple started in a garage. Facebook started in a dorm room. Walmart started as a five and dime. Fast-laners, however, rarely start anything small.

It's great to have big vision. The challenge is there is absolutely no shortcut for mastery, and mastery of anything is a function of time and experience. Many young professionals disrespect the value of time and experience, so they show contempt for the small beginnings.

There's no time to lay a strong foundation in your journalism career because you've set your sight on producing for first solo segment. There's no time to build a solid dating relationship because you're scanning your checklist to see if he is "The One." Whatever literary accomplishment you've made in the moment is seldom good enough because what you really need is a *New York Times* bestselling book to say you're somebody.

What you don't realize in the quest for speed is that you may be ill-equipped to handle your success. Bianca was a young foreclosure expert with a business to help homeowners having trouble paying their mortgages. Many years ago, Bianca learned the lesson about speed in true fast-lane fashion (you know how we do it!). She secured sponsors to launch a nationwide sweepstakes for homeowners and the prize was a full year of mortgage payments for the lucky winner. Bianca thought it would be a great idea to get tons of publicity for her growing business. She recounts:

"When I did the sweepstakes, my energy was crap, my money was crap, my focus was crap, but I wanted to do this thing. It was funny because somebody told me not to do the sweepstakes, and I thought, 'What are you talking about? Of course I'm going to do the sweepstakes! Of course! It will be great!'

"If I hadn't done it, I wouldn't have lost so much money and needed to start over, but I'm glad I did because it showed how little foundation there was under what I was doing. You are the foundation of your business. If you are not happy, healthy, strong and focused, then you may be able to pull things off for a little while, but you

> ### *Conversations in the Fast Lane*
> ### *...on Your Competitive Advantage*
>
> ✓ When you trace your fears or evaluate any counterproductive behavior, do you find it rooted in these two main questions: "Will I be loved?" and "Am I enough?"
>
> ✓ In your past, did you generally believe you were intrinsically worthy or did you aggressively seek to be validated?
>
> ✓ In what ways does the "need for speed" show up in your life, positively or negatively?
>
> ✓ Which of the character values listed in "Character Matters" come easiest for you? Which do you think you will need to work on?
>
> ✓ In the last week, to whom have you compared yourself? How did it make you feel and what resulted from it?

can't sustain yourself for the long run.

"The same goes for your business. If you don't have the foundation of a strong plan and a good idea that has taken time to develop, that you know every part of and can talk about it in your sleep... If you don't have a good financial base for it and the foundation of all the small things that take a long time to pull together, then you're totally building on sand. Everybody wants the flash, but if there is no foundation to your flash, the flash goes away and then—BOOM!—you're left with nothing."

I'm all about making quantum leaps in life with smart strategies in your career, sports, love, money and any other area that's important to you. I highly suggest you make the investments in coaches, trainers, programs and resources to do the same. What you cannot shorten is gaining experience. Contrary to what many believe, experience is not always a function of time or age; it is a function of, well, experience... the actual *doing* of the thing.

Regardless of your title or income, when you know deep down that you are not seasoned in your work, you will feel insecure about your value in the marketplace, even when great opportunities come your way. When you know that you are not seasoned in a relationship, you may question whether you're with the right person, even as you're zooming along to the tune of wedding bells.

By "seasoned," I don't mean certifications and degrees, necessarily, though that could be a part of the measure for you. Bianca went back for her MBA as a result of her sweepstakes experience. I'm talking about taking the necessary steps to work right—not harder, not smarter, but *right*. When you do that, you avoid the meteoric ascent to stardom followed by the fizzle that comes when you've burned out of fuel.

Speed is good, just not at the expense of doing things right. Speed is good, just not at the expense of quality. Speed is good, just not when you're speeding out of fear of some loss. Check yourself and truly evaluate the quality of your outcomes, and make the conscious decision to slow down if you find those outcomes flawed.

As you embark on your career, decide that you're in it for mastery. Mastery is not fly-by-night. If you take the time to read the biographies of venerable superstars and others you admire, their timelines will show that it took a heck of a long time for them to become an "overnight success." And those who opt for the shortcut rarely (if ever) have staying power. Your mind may assault you with thoughts like, "I'll miss out. Somebody will take my spot. They'll beat me to the punch!" But that couldn't be farther from the truth. There's always enough—for you and everybody else.

If you do your part with integrity, you'll be where you need to be at the right time, and you won't miss any achievement that truly belongs to you. I'm not going to say it always feels or looks like that in the moment because sometimes you will feel cheated, passed over, delayed or denied. Just because you feel that way in the moment, doesn't make it true. Even if you have been legitimately cheated, passed over, delayed or denied, it simply means that was not the perfect opportunity for you, no matter how badly you may have wanted it.

As with everything else shared in this book, you have a choice to believe and apply it. If you choose to subscribe to a scarcity mindset that says someone else's success will be at your expense, you'll always feel afraid of missing out, and there will always be another spot for somebody else to take. You'll be driven your whole life by an imaginary need for speed. It will never end and, yes, it will suck. But that's your choice.

My advice: Slow down so you can speed up.

"Success is neither magical nor mysterious.
It is the natural consequence
of consistently applying the basic fundamentals."
— Jim Rohn, motivational speaker, entrepreneur

SECTION 5
••••
Fundamentals of Turning Pro

IN CASE YOU haven't figured it out yet, going from college to the real world means playtime is over.

You're turning pro.

And if you're going to make it in the big leagues, you gotta do what the pros do. That's what this book is all about—helping you turn pro. Every pro, whether they be in sports, medicine or music, will tout the importance of mastering the fundamentals. Most of us prefer to skip the basics and move right on to the good stuff. I get it—there's nothing sexy about the basics. There's nothing sexy about practicing a hundred forehand shots an hour, five days a week. Nothing sexy about line drills, nothing sexy about playing musical scales. There's also nothing sexy about showing up for work on time, being diligent and dressing the part—every single day. But if you want to be a pro in the workplace, you have gotta suck it up and, well... *be a pro*.

You can ignore the basics for a time and still *look* like a pro, but if you choose to skip the fundamentals, you'll eventually pay the price for playing the role.

Individuality and authenticity are good characteristics of young professionals as a whole, but they can create problems if not properly integrated into your work environment. When you first start, you want to do three things: watch, listen, learn. Spend a lot of time observing your colleagues and your bosses. How do they interact? Is there a lot of social interaction at lunch and outside of working hours, or do people largely keep to themselves? Is it a conservative culture? How do people dress, formally or informally? Do people call each other by their first names or do they address each other by their titles (e.g., Ted, Susan, Dr. Thomas, Ms. Smith)?

Pay attention to what you see and begin to mirror the people around you. Mirroring people doesn't mean you lose your individuality. What you are doing at this stage is learning how to build commonality. People like other people who are *like them*. Yes, the corporate world touts diversity, and to a large degree that is true, but even in our diversity, there must be some element of sameness for people to feel comfortable and embrace you. You may not change your gender or your race, but you can adjust small things that help you build rapport and connection with your colleagues.

Remember: You're the new kid on the block. It's your job to adjust to *them*; it's not their job to adjust to you. Take your observations one step further and ask your supervisor or mentor if there are any unwritten office norms that you should be aware of. Be whoever the heck you want to be outside of the office, but master being an "insider" in the office.

I can imagine the protests and "side eye" as you read these words. Yes, your individuality is important, but in the beginning of your career, fitting in with the office culture is much more important than you being you. For a summer intern, doing your best to fit in and not buck the system is non-negotiable. It's only a few weeks, suck it up. If you're a new college hire and you've decided that is not the work environment for you, roll out. But if you have your sights on a long-term career there, you have got to play the game right.

When you have demonstrated your value and exceeded performance expectations, which could take a couple years, to be honest, then you can start bucking conventions where appropriate. Even then, you want to exercise wisdom and ensure your performance is beyond reproach. At that point, the organization will value your contributions more than your conformity to company norms.

Until then, "when in Rome. . . ."

INSIDER SECRET #24
Early Is the New "On Time"

"If you're early, you're on time. If you're on time, you're late."
—LIK HOCK YAP IVAN, philosopher

A recent YouGov survey revealed 22 percent of millennials admit to arriving chronically late to work, and we all know millennials aren't the only ones. People joke about being late. It's become acceptable and in some circles, even expected, to be "fashionably late." I'm telling you to bunk all that and, moving forward, let Ivan's opening quote rule how you manage your time.

I don't subscribe to the idea that you have to be the first to show and the last to leave the office since face time doesn't equate to productivity. Nonetheless, it's crucial that you be on time—for everything—independent of what everyone else in the office does.

During one of my jobs at the start of my career, I would arrive at the office generally five minutes late every day. I didn't think much of it until I got my first evaluation and my supervisor cited punctuality as a development area on my performance review. I was exceeding my performance numbers so I thought to myself, "Dude! It was like five minutes. Seriously?"

The reality was that most people around my cubicle dragged in after I did. But those people didn't have my boss, and little did I know that my boss would stroll the hall at exactly 8:30am most days to see if I had arrived. Yes, he was a bit of a tightwad, but at the end of the day I needed to be on time and not doing so left the impression that I was less than professional and perhaps unreliable in the clutch. Showing up on time really is the easiest part of any job.

At the early stage of your career, you're likely the least proven and probably the person with the least to offer in terms of experience and skills. So you must compensate for that deficit with effort and excellence. One way to do that is to be on time—to meetings, to conference calls, to everything—even if you are the only one there.

Here's the twist to this insider secret: being on time is not sprinting in just under the buzzer, huffing and puffing and exclaiming, "Made it!" No, to be on time is to be *early*. If there's a staff meeting or conference call scheduled, you check in five minutes *early*. If you have a meeting with your boss, show up five minutes *early*, though you might respectfully wait outside his/her door until your designated meeting time. If you're meeting clients, attending a conference or have external meetings, arrive a minimum of 15 minutes early, seated and ready to go.

This secret isn't just about "not being late." There are gems of success hidden in actually being early. Not only will you avoid being stressed so that you can show up clear-headed and ready to shine, but when you arrive early, you'll be one of the few people actually in the room! The only others present will be the host or leaders of the event (and other go-getters you should be connected to and want to network or get to know anyway). You can start one-on-one conversations with key colleagues in ways you would not normally be able to do. This is how you start to set yourself apart—in a good way.

When you are early, you have a captive audience. *Sweet!* Alternatively, you can offer your assistance to the leader or the host of the meeting, and as we talked about in the "Hugs and Handshakes" section, serving influential people is a great way to increase your visibility so the people who should know you, do know you.

One of my coaches, James Malinchak, often talks about the benefit of arriving early to business events, citing that his best deals are done in what he calls the "hallway to riches." He arrives early with a cup of coffee to pick and choose whom he wants to meet and connect without the competition that comes with being a part of the late-arriving masses. When you're just "on time," you miss all these benefits, yet these are the slight advantages that the super successful design for themselves. They are essentially creating their own opportunities by showing up to life ~~on time~~ early.

INSIDER SECRET #25
Dude... Show Up!

"A bad hair day is not a valid excuse for calling in sick."
—TADAHIKO NAGAO, author, *Kokology: The Game of Self-Discovery*

There are only three reasons why you should be taking time off at this stage in the game:

1.) You are actually sick. I'm referring to the contagious, I'll-spread-germs kind of sick. The I'm-sick-of-this-job kind of sick doesn't cut it. Neither does the World-Cup-finals-air-at-1-o'clock excuse;

2.) You have scheduled time off through your manager in advance;

3.) Somebody really close to you died.

That's kinda it. You don't wake up one sunny summer morning and decide that you're not well enough to go to work, though you might be well enough to spend the day on the beach! Yeah. . . no, don't do it.

If you are a new graduate hire and have accrued enough vacation time (see your company guidelines for how that works), you've earned the right to use your vacation time however you choose so long as you have pre-arranged that time. If you're an intern, you don't have much (if any) pull to take time off during your apprenticeship. You don't have any entitlements. This isn't your job, it's your internship. Your work *is* your vacation, so make the commitment to work your full term unless there are extenuating circumstances.

One of the mistakes I made as a young professional is that I didn't consider the impact of my vacation choices on the cycle of the business. I made my plans (in advance), but I didn't always consult with my managers and ask if the days I had in mind to take off were the best time for the team or department.

On one occasion, I just made my plans, booked my flight to Costa Rica, and basically announced to my manager that I would be unavailable for my pre-determined vacation dates. I was using bona fide vacation time, so I didn't perceive there could be a problem. The problem was that my vacation coincided with a major executive meeting for the launch of a new program I would eventually oversee. In my mind I thought, "Too bad, so sad. . . my tickets are non-refundable!"

On two separate annual reviews, my managers made mention of the timing of my vacation when giving feedback on my performance. I can honestly say both vacations were unforgettably awesome, but knowing what I know now about office politics, perceptions and reputation, I would have inquired with my managers and leveraged their input to determine how I would schedule my trip.

It's possible that both trips would have gone exactly as planned, but discussing my options with my managers in advance would have positioned me as more of a team player with a consideration for the needs of the business instead of the immature and clueless newbie I clearly was at the time!

INSIDER SECRET #26
Work When It's Time to Work

"You can't have a million-dollar dream on a minimum wage work ethic."
—STEPHEN C. HOGAN, co-founder, Soul Armor

Whatever your dedicated hours are for work, work them. While the norm around the office might be to take work home, reply to emails in the middle of the night and other bad habits that make people look busier than they are, the reality is that they're often just unproductive during the day. So when it's time to work... *work!*

• Avoid fooling around on social media during work time, as tempting as it may be. I am as addicted to that blinking red light on my smart phone as the next person, but I tell you from experience that you will waste a lot of time, work much longer hours than necessary and miss out on the fun stuff you should be enjoying *after* work. More than that, you'll look like a total amateur on the job! If you want to be treated like a pro, you've got to act like one;

• No texting and checking email in meetings—not even under the table. You're not fooling anybody, ever. I go so far as to suggest you turn the cell phone off during meetings. It will save you a world of embarrassment when you're asked a question and have no freakin' clue what the team has been talking about the prior two minutes because you were engrossed in a fun email! Don't get caught slipping, even if the meeting is as boring as watching paint dry. It looks bad, it's unprofessional, and bosses remember the clown who wasn't paying attention!

• Minimize personal phone calls and business. Sometimes making a doctor's appointment or returning mom's call is unavoidable, so get it done quickly and get back to work;

• Don't ever—ever, ever, ever, (did I say ever?)—walk around the office or shop with the bluetooth glued to your ear.

This advice is not about cracking the whip, it's about freeing your time so you can fit in all the really cool stuff you want to accomplish with your day, your week, your month, your year. "I don't have time" is the modern day grown-up's chief complaint, but it's often a cop out. Real life will pull you into so many competing directions, but it's your responsibility to reign them in. As Jim Rohn would say, "Either you run the day or the day runs you."

Conversations in the Fast Lane
...on the Fundamentals of Turning Pro

✓ Can you see how to maintain your individuality yet still fit in on the job, or will that be a problem for you?

✓ What's your perspective on early, late and being on time? Based on what you've learned, is there anything you need to change in your personal habits to turn pro?

✓ How much of a distraction does phone, social media and other devices pose to your productivity? Is there anything you need to change to be more professional in this area?

✓ Now that you understand the perceptions of professionalism, how does that affect your personal dress code, even in more casual workplaces?

✓ In the past, have you taken the fundamentals of professionalism seriously or have you poo-pooed it as old-fashioned nonsense?

INSIDER SECRET #27
You Gotta *Still* Dress For Success

"One of my first managers once told me to dress for the job you want. If you're dressing like your manager or the people in the next level of the company, you are probably appropriate for the workplace."
—AMANDA HADDAWAY, author, *Destination World: Success After Graduation*

It's true that many companies are trending toward a much more casual dress code. But here's the deal: there's "casual" and then there's, "Gimme a break." I had a career coaching client, Catherine, who came into the office for our meeting wearing jeans, a ratty sweat jacket and straight "bed head." Seriously? She was a super talented engineer, but once I got a taste of her professionalism in dress, speech and presence, I wasn't surprised her company had laid her off.

Some people expect young professionals to have an overly casual dress code, so take it up a notch, always. Err on the side of overdressing, though that doesn't necessarily mean suit and tie. You still want to fit into the office culture, but you do want to dress above your pay grade.

Many of the clients in the office I consult for have kids in and around my age, and those that don't still perceive me to be far younger than I actually am. I recognize that youthfulness can be a liability, if not properly channeled, so while my consulting colleagues dress all kind of casual ways in the office with their clients, I don't do that. If the "young chick" (me) does that, it might be perceived as unprofessional and my clients could lose confidence in me before I have the chance to build it. I don't always have to step up my dress game and neither will you, but you must be aware of the perceptions of your environment and show up one notch above accordingly.

Is the bias fair? No. Is it real? Yes. Do I get results, client referrals and increased revenue from elevating my personal dress code just a tad? Absolutely!

For older colleagues, a professional appearance is more than a formality. "If you underdress, they'll take it as a sign of disrespect," says Jason Ryan Dorsey, author of *Y-Size Your Business: How Gen Y Employees Can Save You Money and Grow Your Business*. He continues: "The more conservative you dress, the older you'll look, the more experience people will think you have, and the more likely they are to trust you with more responsibility."

I was consulting for a company in Silicon Valley that was trying to win some business with Yahoo. I received a call from the vice president of the office asking if I would come in to have lunch with the Yahoo folks. "You look the part," she said. "We think you'd be the right face to put in front of them and you've got the background we need to showcase."

I had other client commitments the same day as the Yahoo meeting, so I politely declined the invitation. That vice president went to my boss and shifted my client commitments to another consultant so I could represent the organization to Yahoo. There were other consultants in the office available, all of them older and more tenured than me. But senior leadership wanted the person most polished to represent the company in the best light.

They wanted *The Kid*!

> "If you can't measure it, you can't manage it."
> — Peter Drucker, management consultant

SECTION 6: BONUS SECRET!
....
Measuring Up

WE LAID THE foundation on how to think about designing your success earlier in the book. When you start working professionally, whether as a summer intern, new college hire or volunteer, that's when you actually start managing your career. Yes…*you*. So, I will lay out a simple strategy for measuring your workplace experience to ensure you're getting the most out of it. This fundamental of turning pro is so important that I have dedicated a separate space within this section to address the topic. Consider it a bonus.

If you want to have an incredible work experience, you must first get clear on exactly what you expect from your job. What do you want to experience? What skills do you want to build and by what timeframe? Your expectation must take into account what your employer actually requires of you. If you've been hired by the IT department to build databases, it might be unreasonable to expect to be in the field visiting clients with the technical sales team.

But maybe not....

If being in the field with the sales team is really something you want to experience, include that bold wish into your work design. I live by the motto, "If you don't ask, you don't get," meaning, if you don't explicitly ask for what you want, you'll for sure miss out on the chance to get it.

As a young person in the workplace, you often have a lot more leeway than you think to create out-of-the-box experiences. Many established professionals get comfortable in their routine or feel they have so many demands on their life that they don't take time to seek out creative experiences that could add to their skill set and professional profile. *Don't let that be you!* Generally speaking, you have more time and freedom, though if you are a working parent, you might have unique life constraints. No matter your constraints, the point here is to think boldly as you design your success.

As you go through the process of designing your work, keep in mind that you've been hired into the role for a specific task, so success factors in your design should incorporate objectives and goals that, when accomplished, also help your boss, team or department succeed. It's not all about you here, so do not lose sight of that!

So, how does this strategy play out practically on the job?

Take the first week to fully understand your role and what your manager and team will need from you across the internship. If you are already in your full-time career, break down the needs into increments: three months, six months, 12 months. Then map out your initial ideas for what *you* would like to accomplish, learn or experience as you satisfy those expectations.

Next, schedule time with your manager to review your understanding of the expectations, your ideas on how to fulfill those expectations and your "wish list" of experiences. Gain his or her input on how realistic your goals are, the sequence of your goals, and any suggestions or resources they have to improve your plan. Your manager will breathe a huge sigh of relief that you are taking the reins of your own career instead of relying on them to do it for you.

Your supervisors have their own job responsibilities and are accountable to their own managers, so by designing your success you are making it easier for your manager to manage you. They will appreciate you for doing so, be more likely to advocate and open doors on your behalf, and you will stand out among your peers for sure.

Score two points for the *kid!*

A few weeks into your new role, check in with yourself using the questions below to see how things are going. When you design your success, evaluating your progress can reveal a lot about your plan—pro and con. The answers to these questions will reveal if you're headed in the right direction or if you need to make different decisions when the project or internship ends:

If you're answering "No" to a lot of these questions, your results might be a good topic of discussion with your manager or mentor. You can also solicit great suggestions for how to improve in the areas where you may be deficient.

PERIODIC WORK ASSESSMENT
Is this internship or role helping me to…

YES	**Gain clarity on my field of study or future career?** If no, how can I improve this?	NO
YES	**Build my network of contacts (peers, mentors, and people of influence)?** If no, how can I improve this?	NO
YES	**Build a list of advocates who can be positive references to influence my career?** If no, how can I improve this?	NO
YES	**Learn new skills: technical, business, interpersonal?** If no, how can I improve this?	NO
YES	**Add valuable accomplishments to my resume?** If no, how can I improve this?	NO
YES	**Decide if I like this type of work as a future career?** If no, how can I improve this?	NO
YES	**Set myself up for a full-time offer or promotion?** If no, how can I improve this?	NO
YES	**Getting a realistic view of potential employers?** If no, how can I improve this?	NO
YES	**Gain greater visibility in my field or profession?** If no, how can I improve this?	NO
YES	**Am I accomplishing the goals I set out for myself at the beginning of this role?** If no, how can I improve this?	NO
YES	**Hand on heart, does this work really excite and energize me at my core?**	NO

BONUS QUESTION! What specific value or impact have I had on my project, team or company? List specific examples of projects you have completed, deliverables you have met and the resulting impact for your employer. Ask your manager, as he or she may have an even deeper understanding of the value of your work to the business than you do. Add these examples to your resume over time.

Tarik was a research intern. He talked about how he used the questions to assess his performance over the summer:

"I absolutely hate networking with people. I usually don't know what to say and feel so awkward doing it. Every time I went back to the checklist, it reminded me that I was missing opportunities in the internship. Every time I got to question 2, I checked, 'No.' I know it's not because the internship wasn't helping me to build my network. It was because I was too shy to make the effort. I worked really hard and I think I did a good job, but I'm sure I missed big chances with my team to build relationships while I was there that might help me when I graduate. I didn't even get people's emails and contact info when I left. It's a real lesson I don't want to repeat moving forward."

Some elements related to these questions will be out of your control, but as Tarik learned, many of them are within your control. At the end of the day, you are responsible for the results of your career and your life. When you are able to correct your own actions, even when doing so is difficult or uncomfortable, you'll get more of what you want, and you'll reach those goals faster.

I thought it might be helpful to give you a sense for the impact of this personal assessment by sharing my answers after that first summer internship with a technology company my freshman year:

So let's analyze a few of my results:

Question #1: *YES*—I did gain major clarity on my course of study and realized I needed to *change* that major. . . quickly! The next semester, I switched from electrical engineering to industrial engineering, which migrated me more into the people side of technology. Based on my natural talents, it was definitely a move in the right direction;

Question #2: *YES*—Like Tarik, I used to be one of those people who hated networking. I was assertive in school, but I was very insecure and unsure of myself when it came to building personal and professional relationships. Despite my deficiency there, just showing up to work created opportunities to meet seasoned profession-

RENESSA'S INTERNSHIP ASSESSMENT
Is this internship or role helping me to…

(YES)	**Gain clarity on my field of study or future career?** If no, how can I improve this?	NO
(YES)	**Build my network of contacts (peers, mentors, and people of influence)?** If no, how can I improve this?	NO
YES	**Build a list of advocates who can be positive references to influence my career?** If no, how can I improve this?	(NO)
(YES)	**Learn new skills: technical, business, interpersonal?** If no, how can I improve this?	NO
(YES)	**Add valuable accomplishments to my resume?** If no, how can I improve this?	NO
(YES)	**Decide if I like this type of work as a future career?** If no, how can I improve this?	NO
(YES)	**Set myself up for a full-time offer or promotion?** If no, how can I improve this?	NO
(YES)	**Getting a realistic view of potential employers?** If no, how can I improve this?	NO
(YES)	**Gain greater visibility in my field or profession?** If no, how can I improve this?	NO
YES	**Am I accomplishing the goals I set out for myself at the beginning of this role?** If no, how can I improve this?	(NO)
YES	**Hand on heart, does this work really excite and energize me at my core?**	(NO)

als who, 20 years later, I still have relationships;

Question #3: *NO*—I blew it here. I was fortunate to come across those who could advocate for my future, but I had zero clue what to do with those advocates and how to maintain the relationships over time. Definitely a missed opportunity there;

Question #10: *NO*—I answered no to this question because I hadn't set any real goals for what I wanted out of my internship experience. Going in, I was young and didn't really know what to expect. I didn't know what I *could* expect; I was just grateful for the chance to work at a company like that. This might be the case for you as well, and depending on where you are in your career, that might be okay. Don't stress too much if you don't feel totally clear right now. With good advisors and occasional soul searching, it will come with time. In fact, this is a great question to discuss with your manager if you're unclear;

Question #11: *NO*—My internship experience was the complete opposite of exciting and energizing. I absolutely hated the work. It paid really well, there was a future and a guaranteed full-time offer with the company after I graduated college, but I was bored out of my mind and couldn't imagine doing that work for the rest of my life! What was great about that experience is it prompted me to seek out different opportunities the next summer. So, by my sophomore summer, I transferred majors to industrial engineering and landed an internship with Procter & Gamble doing indirect sales for *Cover Girl* cosmetics (right up my alley!). Neither P&G nor indirect sales ended up being my long-term calling, but it was a step in the right direction… Score big for *me!*

As my own personal assessment revealed, you may not answer yes to every question, and not every role you accept is intended to satisfy all 10 criteria above. The point of this exercise (done consistently) is to be aware of whether this role is taking you in the right or wrong direction as it relates to your future. You may leave your experience realizing you never, ever want to do this type of project or work again, as was the case for me, and that's a success, too. That knowledge alone will save you a lot of boredom, frustration, wasted time and money in the long run.

Believe me!

"It takes 20 years to build a reputation
and five minutes to ruin it.
If you think about that, you'll do things differently."
—Warren Buffett, legendary business magnate and investor

SECTION 7

••••

You've Got a Rep to Protect

EVERY OUNCE OF success you have moving forward will hinge on your reputation. A professor makes a recommendation on your behalf; a boss goes to bat for you in a promotion review; a friend introduces you to the woman that could be your future wife... all those scenarios are reflections of who other people believe you to be.

That is the power of your reputation, and you must guard it with all you've got.

Your reputation is your most powerful professional currency, yet it's also the most fragile asset you possess, largely because your reputation is not always about who you really are. It's about who other people *think* you are. One bad move on the job may not totally ruin your career, but you'd better believe it could give your reputation a big black eye and there's no guarantee you'll be offered the time or opportunity to bounce back.

To set the foundation for this section, I want to share with you how your reputation is actually built. Your reputation effectively consists of stories one or more people tell about you. Those stories are based on simple actions but they are not always rooted in the fact of those actions. Instead, the stories, and hence your reputation, are rooted in people's *perceptions* of those actions. One of the best frameworks I've seen on reputation-building came from a company I consulted for called Lee Hecht Harrison, so I'll credit this next example to them.

Let's say the first major assignment you are given as part of your new job is a presentation of your team's findings to the boss of your boss. You nail it! That's the simple action. Your colleagues may then make an assessment of that action. They may say things like, "Wow, you gave a great presentation. I was so impressed." From that assessment, they may give you a label like, "You're a really good presenter." You've moved on from the simple action of giving a good presentation to the label of being a "good presenter." With enough people buying into that label, the next time there's a need for a presenter, your colleagues may say, "Oh, we should have the new hire do it, she's a great presenter."

Through the course of one simple action, you have built a reputation. What's funny about this scenario is you may have been so nervous and insecure, thinking you totally bombed the presentation. Or, at a minimum, you were considering all the ways you could have done it better. That doesn't matter when it comes to reputation. The only thing that matters is how other people assess your actions, whether positively or negatively. That's why actively managing your reputation is so crucial.

Early in my career, I learned this lesson first-hand. It was my second job after college and my boss was going on sabbatical over the summer. In addition to my primary role, I was left in charge as project manager for a web portal our department was launching for our premier clients. My job, among other responsibilities, was to work with the IT department to get this portal running, tested, and debugged.

In full disclosure, I found this project to be mind-numbingly boring, so it was rarely on the top of my daily priority list. Apparently, it wasn't on the top of the IT team's priority list either because they were hard to reach, unresponsive and slow to make progress on the technical specs of the project. I made some effort to get this project moving, but it required a "fire-in-your-belly" kind of energy from the project manager (me) to go beyond normal efforts to mobilize my tech partners to drive it forward.

Needless to say, when my manager came back from sabbatical, I had made woefully little progress. I gave him all the reasons (excuses, really) and challenges I'd experienced with the IT team. My manager didn't really comment on the project at all. In fact, he never asked me about it again. He simply went about launching the portal on his own. The fact that my manager didn't call me out on my failure to complete the project when he returned did not mean there were no consequences to my actions, or lack thereof.

I was a top performer in all other areas of my role, which is probably why I was entrusted with the project to begin with, but I sorely underperformed on this task.

Mine was not a boss who took the time to examine my areas of deficiency and give "feedback" to help me develop them. No, this boss wasn't the boss of second chances; he simply wrote me off on that project and moved on! Despite what my reputation had been on his team, this incident (the action) led to an assessment, which gave me a label and finally a reputation with my boss that I couldn't be trusted with a high-profile project.

Fortunately, I took the initiative to address the situation head-on with my manager, owned my shortcomings on the project and began to heal the big black eye to my reputation. Thankfully, I had built enough reputation capital with my boss prior to that incident to recover from the lackadaisical effort and eventually get promoted.

The reality, however, is that the farther removed people are from first-hand experience with you, the more they will rely on other people's opinions when assessing you. That's why Insider Secret #13 on becoming visible is so critical. The reason I was able to bounce back from this screw-up was because it was contained within the relationship with my boss. He didn't go blabbing my misstep to other managers or the executive team in the performance review. Had he done so, I may have never been promoted. That's why this section on reputation will cover major Do's and Don'ts when it comes to your professionalism on the job. Some of these secrets are obvious and common sense, but sadly, some are not.

It might be great to live in a world where people didn't judge you, but the reality is people judge you every second of the day, especially on the job. Every action you take as a young professional is being assessed, positively or negatively, through your co-workers' lenses. So the do and don't secrets listed in the following chapters are included because of the negative conclusions your colleagues can draw as a result of these actions. You may think little of these actions, personally, but those who have influence over whether you get promoted or offered a full-time job do.

So pay attention.

INSIDER SECRET #28
Google Me

> *"Your brand isn't what you say it is; it's what Google says it is."*
> —CHRIS ANDERSON, journalist

I stumbled across an app called "Timehop." What's great about Timehop is every day you receive old text messages, Facebook posts and social media pictures directly to your phone from one, two, three, even four years ago. For most, that stroll down memory lane is a welcome recall of tender or exciting moments you may have forgotten about. For others, it bears the weight of regret of one drunken night of foolishness or a heated exchange with a best friend.

The point is, what is posted to the Internet never completely goes away, even if you delete it and empty your recycle bin. Somehow, somewhere, there is a chronicle of everything posted about you, so it's important that you make efforts to protect your public presence. Every few months, search yourself on Google, Bing, Yahoo and other search engines. Review what your name and likeness are attached to on social media and make any adjustments you need to keep your professional brand positive.

Moving forward, avoid posting *and being tagged* in any photos or comments that could even remotely reflect negatively on your professional brand. Yes, that includes you in the skimpy bikini nestled suggestively against your boyfriend. Yes, that includes the rowdy, buzzed pic with you and your plastered friends at the sports bar. And it definitely includes any profane rants between you and your ex-bestie on social media. Just don't do it.

This is America—land of the free and all that—and you are free to do anything you want with your social media presence. But if you don't manage your online reputation, you are going to pay for it in far more ways than one. Companies are now putting a lot more emphasis on screening potential candidates by checking their online brand—blog posts, status updates, tweets and retweets, YouTube, LinkedIn, etc. Your social media activity, for many employers, is a reflection of your work habits. Moreover, the more senior you become in your field, the more your personal brand will become a reflection of the company's brand. Your best letter of recommendation can be diminished by a negative search result on the web, so button up your privacy settings and restrict who is able to see what's on your social media platforms.

Even if you are going the entrepreneurial route, you still have to "keep your nose clean" online. Of course, there are celebrities who have made millions as a result of an infamous sex tape, but that's the exception, not the norm, so don't bank on that for yourself! People elect to do business with people they trust and invest in brands they respect, so putting yourself in compromising situations is not the smart move if you want to be successful.

On the other hand, you can leverage social media by using it to add value. When you post tidbits of information related to the business you're in or share positive press releases (sanctioned information) about your company or your clients, you 1.) gain visibility and 2.) begin to position yourself as a positive voice within the organization. People notice that. When you initiate your own blog posts, join professional forums or tweet about professional events you attend, you begin to set yourself apart as a thought leader within your industry, an up-and-coming game-changer. These simple strategies make the "Google Me" secret work for you, not against you.

Side note: Life is big on "payback," and when it comes to the foolish indiscretions of our youth, sooner or later we all pay the price for things we've done and people we've hurt. So, be mindful of your actions, virtually or otherwise.

You can still express an honest opinion or advocate for any cause you choose, even if it is a controversial one, but it is important to consider what you say and do, and how it can be interpreted in relation to your professional and personal brand.

INSIDER SECRET #29
Watch Your Mouth, Part 1

"The tongue can bring death or life;
those who love to talk will reap the consequences."
—PROVERBS 18:21

If you're not careful, your mouth can get you in a whole lot of trouble in the workplace. Failing to watch your mouth can get you fired, sidelined from the most prestigious projects, or blacklisted with little opportunity for promotion. One common area where young professionals blow it and don't realize it is gossiping on the job.

We talk a lot about networking earlier in the book, but unfortunately for many young people, their attempt to network and get to know their colleagues results in gossip. A report by Social Issues Research Center suggests that gossip accounts for 55 percent of men's conversation time and 67 percent of women's, which means there are a lot of people talking about other people—usually behind their backs! Let's keep it real and acknowledge that gossip is juicy, whether it is who's dating whom in the office, who didn't meet their performance targets for the month or who's up next for promotion. Gossip can be positive and negative, but a study found that workplace gossip is nearly three times more likely to be negative. Of course, it's the negative gossip that will be your undoing.

In the research paper "Have You Heard? How Gossip Flows Through Workplace Email," PhD student Tanushree Mitra, wrote, "Organizational gossip is a social process. Some people are actively involved in generating gossip messages ("gossip source"), while others are silent readers of the messages ("gossip sink'"), and there are some who play both roles."

Whether you tend to be a gossip source or gossip sink, steer clear of it in the workplace. If you have nothing positive to say about the person or circumstance being discussed, excuse yourself from the conversation completely. Head to the bathroom, go grab a drink, start a sidebar convo with the person next to you—*something*. It may feel uncomfortable to do that and you may instead be tempted to just sit and say nothing. At least then you're not a total punk. No harm, no foul, right?

Wrong.

Being a silent listener when others are going to town with negative gossip still makes you a participant, and associating yourself with gossipers, even if you are not adding to the colorful commentary, can adversely affect your reputation.

INSIDER SECRET #30
Watch Your Mouth, Part 2

"If you can't be interesting without profanity, let's face it: You're not that interesting."

—MICHAEL HYATT, author and publisher

When it comes to profanity, I'm probably middle of the road on my tolerance level. I'm certainly not a fan of it, but I won't necessarily excuse myself from the table if a colleague drops the occasional S-word. Vulgar and crude jokes, on the other hand, are a complete turnoff to me, and I frankly have an unsavory view of those who engage in it.

Whether you lean towards being a prude or a potty mouth is really not my personal concern. However, if you are showing up to the office as Peter or Paula Potty Mouth and you're thinking it's okay, then I'll need you think again. A recent CareerBuilder survey revealed that 64 percent of employers said they'd think less of an employee who repeatedly used curse words, and 57 percent said they'd be less likely to promote someone who swears in the office.

Really, though, what's the big deal? When asked to elaborate on their swearing views, hiring managers responded as follows:

- 81 percent said the use of curse words brings an employee's professionalism into question;
- 71 percent were concerned with the lack of control it displays; 68 percent believed it shows a lack of maturity;
- 54 percent said swearing at work makes an employee appear less intelligent.

Just because everybody in the office is "cool" or because your boss drops an F-bomb or two doesn't mean you get a pass.

I attended a business seminar a while back and went out to dinner with a group of my colleagues, all guys. When the juice started pouring (literally, juice—I'm not even talking alcohol here), boy did they a let it rip! They told some of the nastiest jokes and the language was foul as could be. I get that men hang out differently than women, but they were way over the top, and I made a decision that I would never "hang out" like that with them on business trips again.

Even when the seminar was in session, one guy in particular, Joe, cussed like a sailor, even to colleagues he'd just been introduced to for the first time. It was a normal part of his conversation. *Who does that?!?!* I could tell by the facial expressions and later by comments people made behind his back that these people fell in the 54 percent who perceived Joe's swearing made him less intelligent.

Joe and I are cool, but even I had to ask him to tone it down. I also chose to limit the time I spent with Joe for fear others would associate his behavior with me. Even though I liked Joe, the truth is that I would have to think twice about referring client business his way. He wasn't polished and I feared he would offend people I respect.

The same applies to you. The people you work and do business with may be *friendly*, but that doesn't mean they are your friends. It's a *big* difference. You may perceive you're being relatable by cracking jokes on the job when, in actuality, you could be offending the heck out of people. Most colleagues will smile to your face, but the reality is people have different sensitivities and biases that you will never know about. The colleague you're unwittingly offending could very well be an influencer in your promotion review, and not in a good way. Is a cheap laugh or a profane zinger really worth that risk?

INSIDER SECRET #31
Manage Your Emotions

*"When you show up for work,
leave your personal problems at the door."*
—ERROL CARRIM, life and leadership development coach

I used to consult for a career coaching company in San Francisco. The receptionist, Diane, was one or two jobs out of college. The vice president and other consultants in the office were very excited about Diane when she first started because she hit the ground running, was eager to help and caught on quickly. A few months into her role, however, I started to hear complaints from my colleagues about Diane. "She's dropping the ball," they'd say to one another. "This project was late." or "That meeting was disorganized." In effect, Diane was slipping on the job.

As I was coming into the office one day, I passed by the receptionist desk and casually asked Diane how she was doing. I noticed her spirit seemed a bit low and she didn't represent the perky, fresh-faced corporate brand we wanted our clients to experience when they first entered the office. She proceeded to relay how sad and frustrated she was about a recent breakup. Her ex-boyfriend was being a jerk, he'd already begun dating other people and their mutual friends were taking sides. She had been really bummed for some time and it was affecting her work.

Something was wrong with that exchange. 1.) Diane and I weren't "friends," we were co-workers; and 2.) I hadn't asked for all that information. This was TMI to the max.

You will go through tough times personally and professionally more than once in your career. Unless that tough time requires you to take time off to regroup, which is perfectly acceptable and expected in extenuating circumstances, then leave your personal problems at the door. The hard truth is that most people don't really care about your personal issues, aside from using it as fodder for gossip.

On the other hand, if you have developed a real friendship with a colleague you trust, then by all means leverage them as a sounding board for advice and support behind closed doors. We're human, not robots, so leveraging a close colleague for support might be entirely appropriate at times. Nonetheless, do not let your personal challenges affect your performance as it did with Diane. Get whatever help you need to pull things together and continue to exceed expectations.

Managing your emotions goes beyond Diane's scenario. It includes but is not limited to mouthing off because of conflict on the job, mumbling under your breath when you disagree with a colleague, or publicly bursting into tears when stress and pressure mount. Unless you are a pro athlete who just won (or lost) the big game, steer clear of the tears. Like it or not, ladies, this especially applies to you; tears on the job can be cyanide to your professional reputation.

INSIDER SECRET #32
"My Bad"

"I don't pretend to be perfect; I've made mistakes just like everybody else. When I have, I've owned up to the mistakes and moved forward."
—CHRIS BELL, former U.S. Congressman

Who you are as a professional will be put to the test many times over in your early years. You'll be put to the test by how you perform under stress, how well you deal with conflict and your ability to innovate independently. There will be no greater measure of your professional character, however, than how you respond when you make a mistake. I don't mean those erasable mistakes you can fix without anyone knowing. I'm talking about the sticky situations that create a war inside your head on whether to tell the truth or lie, accept responsibility or blame shift.

My friend Cheryl shared a story of one of those early crossroads. Cheryl was a program manager for a university and leading a team of students to a conference. She rented a car through the university as she normally did for such occasions. When she emailed the paperwork to secure approval for the rental, she submitted the wrong return date by accident, so the university was expecting her to return the car sooner than she actually did.

> ***Conversations in the Fast Lane***
> *... on Reputation*
>
> ✓ Is there a time when your actions earned you a less than favorable reputation?
>
> ✓ When was the last time you audited your online presence? Are there any changes you need to make online to protect your professional brand?
>
> ✓ Has being associated with gossip—directly or indirectly—ever had a negative consequence for you?
>
> ✓ Have you ever been guilty of oversharing personal information in social or professional settings?
>
> ✓ How well do you manage your mouth and emotions around others? Is there anything that needs to change for you to be even more professional in this area?

On the surface this seems like no big deal to fix, but Cheryl had made a few such mistakes in the past, so she was "skating on thin ice." When the admin followed up with Cheryl, she explained her actual return date and resent her original email to prove the details of her return. The problem is that Cheryl noticed the error in her original email and realized she was wrong. Instead of owning up to the mistake, she *changed* the date in the original email to match her story and forwarded that email as if she had submitted the correct return date all along.

So what could have been a very simple mistake to correct spiraled into something horribly wrong. The university began to question Cheryl's integrity. If she could lie about something so simple, what else was she covering up? This issue didn't just stop with the admin and finance team; it went all the way up to the university president.

Cheryl eventually left the school, not solely for this issue, but in part because not owning her mistake left a blemish on her professional reputation. It was no longer a supportive working environment. Her integrity was often questioned, even when she was in the right. So the best option to protect her career was to leave. Fortunately for Cheryl, she was able to move on and she now has a thriving career as a director at another university. But she will forever remember the lesson learned.

A time will come when you will be at a fork in the road of your own screw-up. The decision you make—to lie or tell the truth, accept responsibility or blame shift—will shape the next steps of your career, as well.

"Distinction, quality, superiority, brilliance, greatness, merit, caliber, eminence, preeminence, supremacy, skill, talent, virtuosity, accomplishment, mastery. In other words—excellence."
— Merriam-Webster Dictionary

SECTION 8
••••
Top of Your Game

WHEN YOU THINK of people of excellence, you may envision athletes such as baseball slugger Bryce Harper or tennis champion Serena Williams, singers Carrie Underwood or Lady Gaga or innovators Mark Cuban and Mark Zuckerberg. Without question, these folks are at the top of their game in their respective fields, but they mastered the habits of excellence long before you or I knew they existed.

Former U.S. Secretary of Health, Education and Welfare John W. Gardner wrote, "Excellence is doing ordinary things extraordinarily well." Before the glitz and glamour, promotions, money, title, status and influence, you must demonstrate a willingness to do the ordinary things extraordinarily well. Excellence on the job is about attitude—it's about doing the least sexy tasks as if they were the most high-profile projects in the department. Excellence goes beyond the basic expectation. Not to be confused with perfection, excellence is even reflected in how you ask for help and accept responsibility for your mistakes.

No matter what kind of big man (or woman) you were on campus, what your GPA was or how prominent your parents might be, in the world of work you're a nobody. You're on an even playing field with everybody else and that can be good news or bad news, depending on where you're starting out. Wherever you find yourself, my goal is to give you a competitive advantage as quickly as possible and set you apart…to get the full-time job offer, the high-profile project assignment, the invitation to the emerging leaders program, or just greater connectivity and visibility with people of influence.

If you apply the following secrets to your daily, weekly and monthly routines, you become indispensable—to your boss, your team, your customers—and in no-time you will find doors opening for you that you never expected. You, too, will be at the top of your game.

INSIDER SECRET #33
Understand What Is Expected of You

"There is nothing so useless as doing efficiently that which should not be done at all."
—PETER DRUCKER, author

Here's a truth you must embrace right away: You get paid to deliver results on the job, whether that result is a software program, a spreadsheet analysis or the sale of a product. You don't get paid for how hard you work, your positive attitude or being a great team player. Those are important qualities for a professional, but you don't get paid for any of that. You, my friend, get paid to *deliver*.

So, how do you set yourself up to deliver? Within the first few days on the job, schedule a meeting with your boss to accomplish the following:

1.) Job Description—Make sure you and your boss are in agreement on your role and responsibilities. If you don't already have a job description, ask for one. If you are interning, don't be surprised if a job description doesn't exist; few bosses have time to create one before you start.

If that's the case, write your own job description based on your understanding of the role and ask your manager for his or her edits, or confirmation. Don't overcomplicate this. A simple typed document will do;

2.) Success Factors—Know how your boss defines success in your role. What are the top areas that you will be assessed on, and what does it mean to meet and exceed expectation? There may be a performance review already in place, but if there's not, make sure you jot this information down for your own records;

3.) Get Clear on Their Communication Style—Ask your manager for his or her preferred mode of communication. Do they want scheduled, recurring meetings for you to update them on progress? If so, how often? Would they like brief email summaries? How should you filter questions to them?

A lot of managers are so busy they don't have time to oversee your career. Truth is, they are not responsible for managing your career or your performance; *you are*. And the first step in managing your career is to understand what's expected of you.

INSIDER SECRET #34
Exceed Expectations

"Always deliver more than expected."
—LARRY PAGE, co-founder of Google

Once you have learned what's expected of you. . . do it, then figure out how to produce even more. If "meeting expectations" is 90 percent, make it your goal to hit 93. If the project is due Friday, submit it on Wednesday, asking for any last-minute edits or input. If your workload is light, find an abandoned project that you can sink your teeth into or help a co-worker meet their deadline.

If you do what's asked of you within the timeframe you agree to do it, you'll build a reputation for integrity and reliability. If you go beyond what's asked of you and do it ahead of time, you'll wow people. Wow enough people and you'll build an army of allies who will go to bat for your promotion and advancement. Wow enough people enough times and you'll earn yourself a "get out of jail free" card, redeemable for that inevitable moment in every young person's career when you screw up.

…Exceeding expectations is how you "drop the mic" on your success.

INSIDER SECRET #35
Model the Best

"Success leaves clues."
—TONY ROBBINS, peak performance motivator

When I started consulting for a company, I was the youngest person in the office. Every other person in my specific role was at least 15 years older. While I brought youth, innovation and fresh energy to the group, I knew I still had a lot to learn from those who had been there longer. One of the first questions I asked my boss in our initial meeting was, "Who are the best performers in the office? Who should I model and get to know?" What I did with that question served me well in that role.

Success leaves clues, and if there are standout colleagues who are doing or have done your same role, ask for time with them to understand how they get the job done. Shadow them if it's appropriate. Ask for their templates and blueprints. Ask for advice. Build a relationship with them and offer to treat them to lunch if you can (remember "Hugs & Handshakes" from Section 2). You'll uncover best practices and shortcuts to master your skill and accelerate your achievement.

What I'm suggesting might feel uncomfortable and you may be afraid of rejection, but what few young professionals realize is people are willing to help you… when you're *young*. This same strategy is a whole lot harder to employ when you become more established. As you get older, people might view you more as competition or a distraction and may be less willing to offer their time. So, milk this strategy for all it's worth in the early years!

Keep in mind that not all coworkers perform equally; the friendliest guy in the office might be the poorest performer. Return the dude's kindness but don't copy his work product! Only model yourself after the best.

INSIDER SECRET #36
Master the Fundamentals

"Wax on… wax off."
—MR. MIYAGI, *The Karate Kid*

The opening quote is a famous line from the 1984 hit movie, *Karate Kid*, a pop culture favorite. The principles from the movie are classic for anyone looking to succeed at any goal or dream. In the movie, Daniel is the new kid who gets bullied by the pretty boy high school thugs at school. During a routine beating one night, Mr. Miyagi, an old Japanese maintenance man in Daniel's apartment complex, comes to his rescue and teaches those punks a lesson or two—martial arts style. Blown away by the old man's skills, Daniel asks Mr. Miyagi to teach him karate so that he can defend himself. Mr. Miyagi agrees.

To begin, he asks Daniel to start waxing his collection of antique automobiles, using a strict, circular motion. "Wax on … wax off," he'd say. "Wax on … wax off." After hours of waxing cars, Mr. Miyagi asks Daniel to sand the floor, then later paint a large fence, all while using strict and specific motions … "Side to side… up and down…

" and so on. This goes on for most of the movie. This is not what Daniel had in mind!

Daniel fails to see any connection between his karate training and these hard chores. He eventually gets aggravated, believing he's learned nothing of karate and, instead, is being used as a lackey for Mr. Miyagi's grunt work. When Daniel blows up in frustration, Mr. Miyagi schools him, revealing how all the while he's been learning defensive blocks through muscle memory by performing the chores. In the final scene of the movie, Daniel goes on to face the toughest, most skilled karate student in the All-Valley Karate Tournament Championship. That karate student also happens to be Daniel's biggest bully at school. Who wins? I don't even need to answer that question, do I?

No one achieves greatness without undergoing their own version of "wax on, wax off." Pro basketball star Robert Horry once said this of teammate, the legendary Kobe Bryant:

"I hope the young kids would want to watch him and learn that you can't get anywhere unless you put in the work, the time, and the effort. And that's what Kobe does, he brings a lot of the time, and a lot of the effort... People don't know that, but he's always the first in the gym, and the last to leave, even though he is the best player in the game right now."

And so it must be with you. To be at the top of your game, you must master the fundamentals. No matter what you choose to pursue, you'll have to fiddle with the fundamentals long after your patience has "left the building." Progress almost always takes longer than you anticipate in the beginning, especially for the "high-speed generation" inundated with so many examples of people who seem to have skyrocketed their way to fame, fortune and five million YouTube followers.

...But things aren't always as they "seem" (and that's a chapter for another book).

The point is that if you've grown accustomed to getting what you want *now-now-now-now-now*, you may be tempted to quit the fundamentals and move on to your next big thing, but don't do that. You'll just have to get back in line and start again.

Instead, ask yourself, "What are the fundamentals of your job—the basic, not-so-sexy repetitions that nobody applauds? What are the fundamentals of your business? What are the fundamentals of being a professional?" (Hint: Go back to the section on turning pro.)

If you master the fundamentals, success will take care of itself.

INSIDER SECRET #37
Bloom Where You're Planted

"Bloom where you are planted."
—MARY ENGELBREIT, artist

Congratulations on landing your new job! (If you haven't landed your role yet, it's coming, so congrats in advance!) The surprise, however, is that this role may not be all it was cracked up to be. If you're interning, you might find yourself doing a whole lot of grunt work you think can't possibly be related to your major. If you're one or two years into full-time work or entrepreneurship, you might be wondering why in the world you're repaying student loans for this crap! In either case, you work might indeed suck…until you apply Insider Secret #40.

At this point, it's inconsequential whether you like your job or not; your feelings really don't matter. You always have the option of finding another job or relocating, but as long as you're on assignment, don't half-ass it. Bloom wherever you are planted and leave the mark of a champ. That level of professional integrity will open the most unexpected doors for you. But what exactly does it mean to bloom where you're planted?

Blooming where you're planted answers any one of the following questions:
- What problems can I solve that other people don't seem to have time for?
- What's broken that I can fix—inside or outside of my role?
- Are there situations or processes that really need improving? Can I do something about that?
- How can I make my boss look good or help my team function better?
- Who can I offer to help even though they haven't asked?
- What else can I find to do (a frequent question you might have to ask as an intern if the well of work runs dry)?

When I was in college, I interned for Procter & Gamble, managing *Cover Girl* cosmetics accounts for grocery and department stores. It was the coolest job ever at the time! The full-time sales people were fairly old school. They were all equipped with laptops (no smart phones at the time), yet they recorded their transactions and inventory with pencil and paper, and gave presentations to the store managers by manually flipping paper binders. I thought, "Who does that?!?!"

I began creating digital presentations to use with the store managers in my territory, and I developed automated spreadsheets to track the inventory and other details for my stores. I shared my "innovations" with my manager and he invited me to give a presentation on my best practices to the other reps at the next regional sales meeting.

I wasn't tasked with digitizing the tracking process nor was it in my job description. I didn't understand the point of what I thought was a ridiculously archaic business process, but I also didn't complain about it or talk trash about my old school colleagues who did. I performed my job as I was trained and considered ways I might make my own work better. I had no ambitions of "turning that place around." I simply brought all of me to the job, including some pretty cool ideas and innovations, and somebody took notice.

I moved on from that role, as you will eventually move on from yours, and I can honestly say I bloomed where I was planted while there. Independent of whether you like your role or not right now, make sure that, in the end, you can say the same for yourself.

INSIDER SECRET #38
Ask For Help

"Be strong enough to stand alone, smart enough to know when you need help, and brave enough to ask for it."
—ZIND K. ABDELNOUR, author

"One of the biggest challenges is that young people make all types of mistakes at work," said Tim, who used to be a senior consultant for a major consulting firm. "They wait until the last minute to ask for help because they are afraid of looking dumb. When it's all said and done, they get managed out, and the primary reason they get managed out is because they could have asked for help, but they didn't feel comfortable doing so. I wish I could say the number of times I saw that scenario unfold. For me, that is the No. 1 challenge I see for young people—they need to know that it doesn't make you weak to ask for help."

Be willing to ask a lot of questions when you're starting out in your career. This is another one of those "privileges of youth." People expect you to ask questions; leaders actually get more concerned if you don't have questions. If you don't ask, they will assume you've got things under control and will be less likely to check in and confirm. Remember, your manager has a lot on his or her own plate, and babysitting you isn't one of them.

There really are no "stupid questions," but if you haven't thought through your questions and taken a concerted effort to find the answers on your own, you may end up looking stupid. So take the time to research the answers to some of your questions on your own or identify other people who might be able to answer your questions outside of your boss. Can the admin help you or the IT guy? Does someone on your team know the answer? If push comes to shove and you are still not clear, don't waste too much time. Go straight to the source. Your manager would rather you ask for clarification or support than to spend hours of time producing a wrong result.

Bonus tip: If you ever feel uncomfortable asking a question or seeking out help, simply say, "This might be a simple question, but…(insert your question)." Inevitably, the other person will say, "Oh no – it's not simple at all," and will proceed to help you out. Works like a charm every time!

INSIDER SECRET #39
Get Visible

"It's not who you know, it's who knows you."
—DAVID AVRIN, author

A major mistake professionals and entrepreneurs make is assuming that being good at what they do is good enough. Being good at what you do is expected. Being excellent is better, but just sitting on the sidelines doing great work won't cut it. Other people must be exposed to the value you contribute to the workplace and the world around you.

You *must* get visible.

Getting visible doesn't mean you go around bragging about your latest accomplishment. In fact, the less you actually say about yourself, the better. A *Bible* proverb reads, "Let another man praise you, and not your own mouth; a stranger, and not your own lips." So, gaining visibility isn't about talking yourself up. It's about being in the right places to add value so that your value can be seen.

Getting visible was an area where I majorly blew it during and after college. In fact, I probably hid behind every rock I could to avoid being seen. I remember sitting in a mid-year performance review with my manager. She said that I was doing great work in my role but that other managers who weighed in on the promotion conversations didn't know of me. In order to set me up for promotion consideration in the next six months, she would do her part to advocate on my behalf, but I had to get more…you guessed it…visible within the leadership team.

It was the very thing I was reluctant to do, but money talks, and I got myself into gear! Fortunately, I got promoted the next go-around, but I have no doubt I missed a wealth of opportunities personally and professionally because I was slow to accept the reality that career advancement is a "contact sport."

Over the years, you may watch your peers and colleagues promote themselves when, in actuality, their work product is less than stellar. They'll take short cuts and they may cheat, but they will advance more than you because they are *visible*. To avoid that kind of letdown, make it a point to learn how to get visible in your field. Here's how:

Join Organizations—Join a professional association, alumni group, non-profit or volunteer organization you believe in. So many opportunities avail themselves when you just show up to things;

Lead—Join the *leadership team* of these organizations. Don't just sit on the sidelines as a card-carrying member. One strategy is to assume leadership in an area that caters to your strengths and adds value. You'll be able to hobnob casually with more senior and established professionals and you will gain access to events, lunches and behind-the-scenes activities that can elevate your profile. A ninja strategy, however, is to participate on the membership committee of an organization. That's not always the highest profile role, but it is the "broadest" profile role with fantastic access. You get to meet and interact with *everybody*, typically in a less intimidating way, and you already have a built-in and legitimate reason to engage them. This strategy is truly brilliant!

Attend Annual Conferences—Most professional organizations associated with your major or field have college or young professional chapters and annual conferences. Go to the conferences! Yes, they do cost money, and even the discounted student or "yo pro" rates can feel like a stretch on your pocket. Depending on the

> ## *Conversations in the Fast Lane*
> ### *... on Being at the Top of Your Game*
>
> ✓ Do you typically just aim to meet the expectation set for you, or do you go the extra mile to exceed expectations?
>
> ✓ Whatever your immediate goals, whose performance can you model to improve your own?
>
> ✓ Do you ever get discouraged because you feel like you're stuck mastering the fundamentals in school, on the job or in your business?
>
> ✓ In what ways can you bloom where you are planted right now and how can that perspective impact how you do your work?
>
> ✓ In what specific ways can you get more visible in your program or job?

• •

event, you might be able to persuade your boss to invest the company's dime to sponsor you. It's worth a try to ask, but even if your boss declines, attending is worth the investment if you can swing it. Established professionals tend to be welcoming and eager to connect with younger professionals, so being present at these types of events are invaluable to your career. It will give you a leg up on your peers if you work it right! Not attending is a major missed opportunity;

Socialize With Colleagues—Whether during internship or your full-time job, when the opportunity arises to go out and have fun with colleagues, do it! This is how you get to know people on a casual level, create memories and the ever-bonding "inside jokes." This is <u>not</u> the time to get high, drunk or join a gripefest about your boss. Instead, use this time to make friends and listen for opportunities to meet their needs, not just your own;

Do Lunch—A subset of the tip above, avoid the temptation to eat lunch at your desk by yourself. Instead, make plans to go out with co-workers, even if only to the company cafeteria or the local food truck. If you're in a company with few interns or recent college hires, having lunch with established professionals might feel intimidating but try to push past the discomfort. It really will get easier. On the other hand, avoid sticking with your intern or new-hire clique. Yes, you are technically "doing lunch" when you go out with your intern clan, but you are missing a big opportunity to broaden your network if you stick within the comfort zone of your peers;

Participate—Participate in those seemingly insignificant events with your company that have nothing to do with your job, such as the volunteer events, 5k charity walks and holiday party committee. To manage your time, choose events you actually have an interest in, but participate nonetheless. These are great opportunities for you to make connections outside of your department, add value and even get your photo on the company website, intranet or newsletter. All of this sets you apart and gives you easy opportunities to gain visibility;

Social Media—Start a blog for your ideas or post meaningful comments on social media within your field or profession;

Step Up—When a high-profile opportunity comes around, put your name in the hat, even if you fear you won't get chosen. If you don't get the role, gather some feedback for improvement and apply for the next opportunity. Don't get twisted about the failure of it all; it honestly doesn't matter if you're selected or not. Over time you'll gather name recognition, especially if you are a quality employee, and that's professional currency. People will begin to notice you and start earmarking you for opportunities before they even become public.

Just the thought of some of these ideas may terrify you, but, remember, it's not who you know that counts; it's who knows you. And people don't necessarily need to actually know you, they just need to know *about* you. So, show up to life, participate, ask questions and contribute. You can't be at the top of your game if nobody else knows you're even in the game!

"Twenty years from now,
you will be more disappointed by the things
that you didn't do than by the ones you did do.
So throw off the bowlines.
Sail away from safe harbor.
Catch the trade winds in your sails.
Explore. Dream. Discover."
— Mark Twain

SECTION 9
••••
Go Big or Go Home

GO BIG OR go home!...Go BIG or go home!...Go BIG or go home!... If you adopt this mantra as the battle cry for your life, there is no telling how far you can go—in career, business, relationships and adventures.

Many people play way too small, settling for what they think they can get out of life instead of going for what they really want. The challenge for young professionals is they think they're playing the game of life in a big way, when in actuality, they aren't.

You may have been the first in your family to finish college or grad school. You might have been heavily recruited for your sports, academics or musical abilities. You may even work for a prestigious Fortune 500 company or a cool start-up—all impressive achievements—but are you really playing big?

Playing big doesn't mean you're always at the top of the leaderboard. No, playing big is...well...*bigger* than that. It's going for the dream that's burning in your heart even if you fear you won't be able to achieve it.

It's asking the girl out when you feel she's way out of your league. It's changing careers mid-stream when you know for sure that passion has "left the building" (and ain't coming back)! It's submitting the application, going on the audition, writing the book, losing the weight, chairing the committee, protesting for what you believe, running for office or taking that assignment in Mozambique.

Erika is a senior director for an educational nonprofit. She recalled:

"When I completed undergrad, I wanted to move to New York, take some classes in makeup artistry and do makeup. My mom flipped out and was like, 'I didn't pay all that money to that university for you to get a degree in microbiology, then go live in

New York and paint somebody's face! You've got to be out of your mind.'

"And so I conceded, 'She's right. I need to do something that makes sense—like go to grad school or get a responsible job.

"But I wish I would have done it. I might have gone to New York, tried it and hated it," Erika continued. "That's okay. I could have tried it, loved it and become a makeup artist to the stars. That's possible. Or, I could have tried it, loved it, realized there were makeup products that I could manufacture even better and thereby gone a slightly different route. Who knows? I could have been the next Bobbi Brown or Michelle Phan. You just never know."

If you ask Erika's mom, she'd say her baby went big! She's a graduate of a respected university and Master's program. She has a good paying job, takes care of herself, and has the resources to take fabulous vacations every now and then. But, Erika would say different.

She'd say she punked out on living her very best life.

Make no mistake—playing big inevitably means you'll lose big at some point. In fact, you'll lose big and be disappointed more than most, but that's because you're taking a lot more swings at the bat of greatness. The greatest team in baseball history is the 1927 New York Yankees of Babe Ruth, Lou Gehrig and the Bronx Bombers. They won 110 games and destroyed their opponents, but they still lost 29 percent of their games. You can't hide from the occasional disappointment, but the disappointment is far outweighed by the opportunity to experience the adventures of a lifetime.

There are no coulda, shoulda, woulda, didn't-do's when you go big. When you go big, you'll end up bruised, bloodied and battered on the road to your "right direction," but you *will* overcome. More than that, you'll have the privilege of looking back on a life with no regrets.

You would have left it all on the court, and that's how fast lane champions do it.

INSIDER SECRET #40
Fail Your Way to Success

*"If it wasn't for those first few failures,
the future successes would never have happened."*
—SIR RICHARD BRANSON, founder, the Virgin Group

There are seven words that represent the core message of this chapter: Make room in your life for failure.

Some fast-laners don't know what it's like to have a tail-spinning, gut-wrenching, lift-your-face-out-of-the-mud kind of failure. Sure, you've had some disappointments, but you've worked hard and somehow things have always worked out—in school, work or extracurricular activities. You've earned your success rightfully, yet there's an intense fear of being out of control and not having a calculated "win."

For others, you may have experienced that kind of failure and vowed to never (*ever!*) go back there again. Either way, when failure happens, or the illusion of failure happens, it feels as if you have been sucker punched. You don't know what to do or how to react. Worse, you're more likely to propel yourself into what you know will be the wrong direction just to avoid the pain of failing. Consider the experience my entrepeneur friend Dolores had when she tossed aside her financial security blanket:

"When I quit my job, I thought everything was going to work out; things had always been really easy for me. But the fact of the matter is that for three and a half years now, I've been working to build a business that has been completely unprofitable. If you had told me when I left that job I wouldn't make enough money to live at the level I was living before, and yet still I would find a way to make things happen, I never would have believed you... and I probably wouldn't have quit my job."

Like Dolores, I didn't make room in my life for failure when I started my first business, so when the business imploded and I lost everything, I saw it as an indictment on my worth. I got back in the saddle and started another business, but the fear of experiencing more failure colored everything I did. It took me years before I could enjoy the freedom of being self-employed because I was so afraid of failing again. That's because I didn't get Insider Secret #43.

As an entrepreneur, I knew failure was an inevitable part of success, but I didn't get that it was a *necessary* part. I didn't know that the teeter-totter of failure and success would actually transform me into the woman I needed to be to succeed at my dream—a dream, I might add, that has morphed over and over as a result of failure.

Who I thought I would be and what I thought I would be doing looks quite different than what I first envisioned, yet it's unmistakably right. Each setback, disappointment or negative feedback either pushed me in a new direction or challenged me to get better. So in hindset, there was nothing to be afraid of. What I thought was failure was actually a compass steering my path; I just didn't understand that secret at the time.

Can you look back at a time in your life where something didn't go according to your plan, only to find out later it was the greatest gift that could have happened to you? It could have been a program that rejected you and changed your course of study, a challenge in your childhood, getting dissed by a lover or bombing on a project. We can all pinpoint something. In that moment, it's a real bummer, but in retrospect we often thank God for that unanswered prayer.

So when you find yourself boo-hooing about your latest disappointment, you may have decided too soon what that experience really means. It could actually be the best thing to ever happen to you. Just give it a minute; you may simply be failing your way to success.

Sadly, most young professionals are mistaken about what failure truly is, so I feel compelled to explain what failure is *not*:

- Failure is *not* being unsure of the answer or what to do next;
- Failure is *not* experiencing criticism or making a mistake;
- Failure is *not* the fact that you feel afraid;
- Failure is *not* screwing up on your first, second or third try;
- Failure is *not* deciding to change directions in favor of a better path;
- Failure is *not* realizing you need to ask for help.

When you have a healthy perspective on what failure is (and isn't), you'll no longer take the stumbles of life so personally. Tripping over yourself in the pursuit of your goals will never, ever feel good, but those who "turn pro" learn know how to pick themselves up and keep moving.

INSIDER SECRET #41
Get Over It—Fast

"Success consists of going from failure to failure with no loss of enthusiasm."
—WINSTON CHURCHILL, former British Prime Minister

When you decide to "go big or go home," you will make a lot of mistakes—guaranteed. Most mistakes will be small ones with minor consequences, but on occasion you will make a colossal mess of things. In the last chapter, we talked about how failure, disappointment and negative feedback can serve as a compass to steer your direction. But failure isn't always an indication that you're off-purpose; it's sometimes an indication of poor decision-making, a lack of preparation or inefficient investment on your part.

In short, you screwed up.

The screw-up is fact, and how you deal with that fact will determine the magnitude of its impact and how long it will take you to get back on track to success.

Older people have a way of putting things into perspective quickly, and one of my mentors, Rosemary, whom I playfully nicknamed my "Oracle," invited me over one night to chat about why I had been in an emotional funk for weeks. As Rosemary began to ask questions, I realized I had bottled up so much shame from what I felt like were major failures in my first real estate business: poor decisions, wasted resources, wasted time and second-guessing. At one moment, I had $200,000 in the bank; the next moment I had a mere $1.97. Retirement funds were gone, stocks were gone, savings were gone.

I had tried for a couple years to reframe those failures because some of those disappointments were indeed indescribable lessons that I got to apply to the next business. But for some reason, I still had this unrelenting whisper taunting my spirit. "You're a fake," it would say. "Who are you trying to fool? You screwed everything up."

I was explaining this to Rosemary when she pointed out bluntly, "Game over. In the business of life, you win some and you lose some. You lost. Get over it."

Wait, what? I lost?

It seems like the simplest of realities, but it was a major breakthrough for me. I understood that in head-to-head competition, there is only one winner. Sometimes you're that winner, other times you're not. For some reason, though, I viewed going after my big dreams very differently. I had been deliberate, I sought advice, I followed direction, I took big risks, I stepped through fear, I made unimaginable sacrifices. I applied a lot of these insider secrets to my own life.

But as Bruce Wilkinson wrote in *The Dream Giver*, "sometimes when you risk everything, you lose everything, too. Or so it seems at the time." Bruce must have been onto something because, at one point, I went from earning six figures to needing my parents' help paying my bills. I had lost everything… *or so it seemed at the time*.

The problem with me losing is I had attached losing with being a *loser*. I had placed so much personal judgment on losing that it took me way too long to accept I had lost. I knew intellectually I had failed, that I had made mistakes, but I couldn't grasp that failure was okay. Because I couldn't grasp that failing was okay, I spent too much time repairing my ego instead of assessing what happened and quickly making my next move.

Yep, I lost a boatload of money. Yep, the first couple of businesses failed. Just as a championship team may lose a game or two on the road to winning the big one, losing is par for the course for bodacious living! I could make more money. I could try the business again. I could do something altogether different. Whatever I did, I first needed to get the hell over it—quick.

Failure is an inevitable part of your success, and the failure pros know how to fail well, fail fabulously and fail *fast*, navigating through the disappointments with no loss of enthusiasm for their dreams. It's an acquired skill and takes time, but when you earn your black belt in "emotional kung fu," there's no limit to what you can achieve!

INSIDER SECRET #42
Never Hide From Criticism

"Never hide from criticism. I like criticism. It makes you strong."
—LEBRON JAMES, basketball legend

If there is a character trait most conducive to failing, it is the fear of criticism. When there's a choice to go big or go home, the fear of being criticized will send you packing every time! Avoiding criticism will paralyze you to the extent you never go after the real desire of your heart for fear you can't do it right. The time would have long passed for you to make an important decision or finish a big project or submit your contest entry because you spent so much time making things just a little bit better instead of learning the art of "good enough." Some of us have this deep, dark place inside that feels we have to be perfect, even when logically we know that's completely untrue. We know it's impossible to be perfect, but we strive for perfection anyway.

In truth, perfection is not about being better, it's about being *enough*. If you are perfect and without flaws, you can't be criticized, judged or rejected, can you? You'll finally measure up, right? Wrong. If you make the commitment to go big, be prepared to stand out, and as marketing guru Seth Godin warns, "Criticism comes to those who stand out."

To go BIG does not mean to go sloppy. Don't do a half-assed job, or rush a deliverable or neglect to do your homework to achieve a great outcome. On the contrary, do what you know to do with excellence, step out there and accept that you can improve along the way.

If you don't believe that works, consider the ridiculous number of technical bugs in the first release of Apple's revolutionary iPad tablet. Bugs didn't stop Apple from being the first to successfully launch a tablet, shouldering a truckload of criticism while pocketing a boatload of cash along the way. Apple isn't perfect, but they go big, so big that we dismiss just how *imperfect* their products are.

Criticism can show up in a performance review on the job or in a friend's feedback of your personality. A coaching client, Sandy, called me out of the blue after receiving her annual performance evaluation. She was blazing mad, upset that she had received lower marks than she thought she deserved. Every review includes development areas, and Sandy overall received a very positive review. However, she felt she wasn't being valued by her boss for how above and beyond she'd gone on the job, and she felt underpaid. She cussed, she vented; there were tears of frustration.

We discussed the specifics of her review and I pressed her on whether the constructive criticism was true or false. Sandy had to admit there was truth to the negative feedback and she had to take full responsibility for the areas where she was less than stellar. She wanted to blame it on the overwhelming workload, or the fact she was often the go-to person for other people's responsibilities. While all that was true, she had legitimately dropped the ball on the areas reflected in her review.

Fast forward to the next day when I received the following text message:

"No matter my evaluation of what I think I've done, the fact is that I'm not that good *yet*, but I will be!"

It turns out that part of the problem was *who* the criticism came from. Sandy was having some interpersonal challenges with her boss and didn't feel as though her boss was advocating for her progress. She didn't particularly like or trust her boss, so the feedback had an extra layer of sting to it. Quite possibly, a different person could have delivered the same feedback and Sandy might have received it better.

The point here is that you might get criticism from people you don't like (and who don't like you!), but that doesn't make the feedback any less valid. Instead of wasting time getting angry, defensive or embarrassed, get curious.

- Is there any truth to what the person is saying?
- Do you need to accept any responsibility?
- Is there a way for you to grow or develop from what they shared?

If you absolutely must get angry, defensive or embarrassed, then go ahead. Go there (*in private*). It won't help much, but at least you'll get it out of your system! Then, like Sandy, kick your pride to the side and assess if there's even a tiny hint of truth to what your critics are saying.

However, one of my clients did the complete opposite.

I was coaching a young man, Ben, who was trying to land a new job in the hot tech market of the San Francisco Bay area. He was a super talented guy, but he had been laid off from his previous company. He was getting loads of first- and often second- or third-round interviews, but he couldn't seem to close the deal to an offer. This had gone on for months, so he came to me for help on nailing an offer and getting back to work.

After several conversations with Ben, I noticed a troubling pattern in how he engaged the companies in his pipeline. I'm all for exuding confidence in the workplace, but Ben thought he was the "cat's meow" and that arrogance was reflected in how he communicated. What's interesting is that Ben's arrogance was really a mask for insecurity, and his insecurity was driven by the fact that...

1.) He had been laid off to begin with;

2.) He'd been seeking employment for months with no success;

3.) And his "money was funny" to the point that he was living off credit cards to support himself.

His desperation to secure an offer made for some premature and off-putting tactics with hiring managers and recruiters. He simply could not fathom why some company had not scooped him up already! Every time he got passed up for a role, he had some explanation, and it was always the companies' fault.

In what became our final coaching call, Ben asked my feedback on how he was approaching his job pipeline. I proceeded to tell him honestly about how his actions might be perceived in the marketplace and what to do to get a different result. I coach on average 150 people a year to land six-figure salaries, so I know a thing or two about how to get results in his market. I paused for a moment in my delivery to ask for Ben's reaction to my comments only to be greeted with silence. The conference line was dead.

For some reason, I knew in my gut this was something I should be really mad about. My mind immediately went there:

"Did this dude just hang up on me?"

I was instantly heated, but there had to be an explanation. No professional in their right mind, especially one who didn't have a job and had been passed over for several jobs, would hang up the phone in the middle of his coach giving him feedback on said job issues! So, I decided to give him the benefit of the doubt, and followed up via email. Surely, we must have gotten inexplicably disconnected!

And here was Ben's reply:

"I hung up. I was not pleased with the direction of our conversation and thought it was a better use of my time to tackle other projects today."

Who the @#$%^! does that?

Ben does that.

Ben does that to his coach. Ben does that on the job…and that's why Ben hadn't landed a satisfactory role in 15 months.

Accepting criticism is hard for all of us. No matter what anyone says, it's always personal. Criticism is saying we aren't good enough or we didn't do something right. There is "criticism" and there is "constructive criticism," but for many people the lines are blurry because all we really hear is we don't measure up.

Your ego might say, "Who do they think they are? They can kick rocks!" But it's not about them, it's about you. It's about bringing your best self to the marketplace to achieve the highest levels of success and fulfillment possible. None of us has all the answers. None of us is perfect. How we accept, handle and grow from criticism is extremely important in all facets of life, especially in the workplace.

The thing is, there is also a widening divide between generations, especially in this age of "helicopter parenting" in which social and cultural traits are often bypassed for individual goals and achievement. Experts claim today's Millennials were raised as "Generation Me," developing into a culture of "trophy kids" with a sense of entitlement. In other words, they can do no wrong. Does this mean today's young people can't be "coached?" Of course not, but my friend Dennis, who spent over 20 years in the newspaper business, says he always looked for coachable personalities when he hired.

"Talent gets you a closer look," he said. "Experience and talent gets you in for an interview. Common sense says hire the candidate with the most talent. But there were times when we found out during the interview or by talking to references that the candidate didn't handle direction very well or they weren't very coachable. No manager wants to deal with a personality clash, so we often hired the person with the best combination of talent and coachability."

Constructive criticism is healthy, even though it can sting. If you're wise, you'll use it to better yourself, your work and your life. Every now and then, you'll encounter people who are downright nasty for no good reason. Their feedback is not constructive and their intention is not for your good. When that happens, as Taylor Swift would say, "Shake it off."

"Cause the haters gonna hate, hate, hate, hate, hate..." Lol.

INSIDER SECRET #43
You Can Figure It Out

"If your dreams don't scare you, they aren't big enough."
—ELLEN JOHNSON SIRLEAF, president of Liberia

I mentioned earlier that one of my favorite books is *The Dream Giver* by Bruce Wilkinson. In that book, Wilkinson recalls a conversation he had with a friend who was a leadership development expert. Wilkinson asked his friend what was the most important secret to developing world-class leaders. The friend replied:

"... To take people out of their safe environment and away from the people they know, and throw them into a new arena they know little about. Way over their head, preferably. In fact, the more demanding their challenges, the more pressure and risk

> ## *Conversations in the Fast Lane*
> ### *...on Going BIG!*
>
> ✓ If you believed you could figure out whatever challenge comes your way, how would that change how you pursue your goals?
>
> ✓ How do you react to criticism? Does a fear of criticism impact your willingness to take risks?
>
> ✓ Do you get over failures quickly or do you stew in disappointment? How is that working for you?
>
> ✓ In what ways can you "go bigger" in your current goals?
>
> ✓ How does the concept of "failing your way to success" change your perspective on how you achieve?

they face, the more likely a dynamic leader will emerge."

If you indeed want to go big in your life, get in over your head and get comfortable being there. Being in over your head will never feel comfortable, but when you consistently challenge yourself to go big despite your fears, you will eventually get comfortable *being uncomfortable,* and that's the trick.

So put your name in the hat for the big project. Chair the program or run for office. Decide to be the lead fundraiser for the charity walk. Do the thing that scares the pants off you; that's when you know you're headed in the right direction, the path that will catapult your success and fulfillment.

The reality is you can always figure things out. Whatever the circumstance, you have what it takes to step back, analyze the situation, get help if you need to fill in the gaps, then move in the right direction for you. You must believe that, even in your most confusing, fearful times. When you stop flailing about chaotically, you will likely discover that you are capable of treading the waters of life and finding your own solution.

When Audrey decided to leave her human resources consulting career and launch a non-profit, she shared:

"I had a reasonable degree of self-confidence that I could figure it out. That's one thing I always believe to be true about myself, and hopefully other people think it's true about themselves, as well. I might not know the answer. I might not have all the resources and the materials. I'm definitely not the smartest cookie in the room, but I trust myself enough to be able to figure it out."

What kept me in a sinking business partnership years ago was that I didn't have the confidence that I could figure out the business on my own. I felt like I "needed" my partner to succeed, so I endured a very dysfunctional relationship far longer than I should have. All of my achievements prior to that partnership were evidence that I could succeed without her, but I had to develop a deeper confidence in myself. Fortunately, that confidence sprang from the pain of that partnership.

Now I have 100 percent belief that I can help anyone with whom I come in contact. There is not a coaching client I can't help or an audience I can't inspire. If there were someone better to serve that client than me, that client would be in front of… someone else. The fact they sought me out for coaching, strategy or motivation is sufficient evidence that I'm their girl!

So, if an opportunity is presented to me and it makes sense, I say, "Yes!" first, confident I can figure out the "how" later. To be honest, sometimes that "how" sounds like, "How in the H-E-double hockey sticks is that going to work out?!?!" There are times I definitely feel way over my head, but trusting this insider secret never fails.

"Enjoy yourself.
These are the good old days
you're going to miss in the years ahead."
— Unknown

SECTION 10
••••
Milk Your Age For All It's Worth

THE OPENING QUOTE is one of my favorite pieces of advice. Sadly and almost without fail, getting to the place where you can simply enjoy yourself in the pursuit of success is a realization most people come to grips with around the time they turn...*hmmm*...50! Pablo Picasso might have been on to something when he said, "It takes a long time to become young."

I am a firm believer that every season of your life can be the best season of your life, but there is one catch:

Seasons change.

I am a summer bunny. I'm for anything that resembles blue skies, sunshine and warm weather, yet as I pen this chapter, we're embarking on the first days of fall. Whatever art festivals, Screen-on-the-Green movie nights or outdoor concerts I missed in June, July and August I can just chalk up to being "S.O.L."

Too bad. So sad.

Every season has its beauty and its adventure, but it also has a very finite window. When it's gone, it's gone, so it's important to make the most of the season you are in. *I mean milk it for all it's worth!* No matter where you are right now—whether you feel like you're in the fast lane going in the wrong direction, the right direction, or with no direction at all—the reality is this season has profoundly powerful potential for you.

Your college years are the season to explore your possibilities. Your 20s are the season to fail fast and fail often. That doesn't mean you go chasing failure; it simply means you generally have the ability to bounce back faster with fewer major consequences. This is the season to push your boundaries, to try on the different "outfits" of life and see which ones fit you best. The good news is you don't have to get it right on the first crack, people *really do* want to help you, and you have less to lose now than you ever will in life.

George Bernard Shaw said, "Youth is wasted on the young," and in some sense he's right. Most people don't know how to enjoy being young. I'm not talking about getting high, sleeping around and drinking your way through Daytona. That's just stupid. I'm talking about squeezing the sweet juice out of your youth and leveraging the right kind of support to make your dreams come true.

Many of us spend our early years insecure, afraid, and unsure of ourselves. We worry about what people think about us and whether we measure up. We worry about messing up. It's not until we wake up and realize what most people think of us doesn't matter; we're already enough in spite of our imperfections and our fear of failure is often way worse than our actual failures. We learn that life can be forgiving and there are lots of chances for do-overs. Unfortunately by then, we're 40-something and wishing we had done our 20-somethings a little bit differently. If only we had a clue.

Well, here's your clue.

I don't know your personal circumstances. You might be footloose and fancy free, with only yourself to be concerned about. You might already be married or with kids. You could be shaking off the residue of a traumatizing childhood, still trying to find your own "voice." Whatever your situation, don't waste your youth.

Enjoy life. These are the good ol' days you're going to miss in the years ahead.

INSIDER SECRET #44
People Actually Want to Help You

"They are the students. I have to help."
—ERICA, San Francisco entrepreneur

I was out to dinner with a Erica, a fellow Stanford alum, when the topic turned to the calls we often get from college students asking us to ante up for our alma mater's university fund. If you have not started getting those calls yet, you will, and if you're one of those students who made those calls back in the day, I apologize in advance!

I am a very generous person, but I admit I hate getting those calls as much as I hate telemarketing solicitations, so I rarely pick up the phone. Erica doesn't like the calls either, but she always lets the students do their spiel. I said it's a waste of time to listen unless you plan on shelling out at least the minimum requested donation, to which she replied, "They're students. I have to help."

And so it is.

One of the biggest advantages of being a young professional is that people actually do want to help you. Despite my aversion to college fundraising campaigns, I like to help young people, too! While I used the example of college students, make no mistake that this advantage applies at least until you're 30. More established professionals are willing to provide you with advice, mentorship, connections and resources free of charge because they often see themselves in you and are either grateful they had similar support when they were building their careers or wish they had.

Right now, you don't pose a threat to their careers; in fact, you sometimes represent a goodwill outlet and your success is payment enough. The more years a person is removed from you and affectionately views you as a "junior," the more willing they are to help. Bump my head, I wish I had known this years ago! This kind of unbridled assistance still happens to me on rare occasion, but it definitely doesn't come from my 30- and 40-year-old peers. I have to reach up to the 50s and 60s for that kind of royal treatment!

Take advantage of this reality because there is a shelf life to this professional goodwill. Just like every cute, 5-year-old "Little Timmy" grows into awkward, 14-year-old "Tim," you become less attractive for the free advice and mentoring gravy train as you age. After a while, you have to start paying handsomely for that insider info, resources and connections just like the rest of us. You'll have to invest a whole lot more into your relationships to extract the same value you get when you're a young gun.

So, if you would like to have lunch with a more established professional or entrepreneur, ask them—and be prepared to treat, if you can. If you'd like to shadow how they run a meeting or an event, ask. If you know someone who can introduce you to someone else you would like to know, ask. Every ask won't result in a yes; in fact, you might get quite a few polite rejections. That's life and you'll get over it. The reality is that people are more inclined to grant you a piece of their valuable time at this stage of the career game—no strings attached—than at any other time moving forward.

INSIDER SECRET #45
Right Place, Right Time

*"Luck is being in the right place at the right time,
but location and timing are to some extent under our control."*
—NATASHA JOSEFOWITZ, author, poet, lecturer

We talked about the importance of getting visible earlier in the book, and this chapter will reinforce why *now* is the easiest time for you to get visible. As I have mentioned, people are willing to help you while you're young but they are not going to go out of their way to find you. You need to be in the right place at the right time, and the right place is wherever your potential mentors and the people you admire are. You've got to show up, take advantage of opportunities to connect, ask questions and, where appropriate, serve.

It's that simple.

When I speak to student groups at colleges, they inevitably have a ton of questions after the presentation about the career direction, choices and challenges they're facing. As much as I love to mentor young professionals, I don't have the bandwidth to take individual emails and personal calls from everyone I meet. So when my calendar allows, I often offer a free group coaching call one week after the event for any student who participated in the conference. It's an opportunity for them to have my undivided time and mentorship, recommendations, resources and connections. I love engaging and encouraging young people.

Considering how many students are clamoring for my time and attention right after a conference talk, you would be amazed how few make the time and effort to get on the group coaching call for more personalized attention. What a wasted opportunity! Obviously, some students have legitimate class conflicts or whatever, but making every effort to get on that call and take the opportunity for personalized mentorship is one example of being in the right place at the right time.

By being on that call, participants receive more personalized advice for their career and life, and I occasionally connect with them on LinkedIn or get to know them better offline. All of those are wins. . . and all you have to do is *show up*. Like, duh! Remember: Even though people are willing to help while you're young, they won't go out of their way to find you.

So, go to the class reunions, the alumni events, the sorority and fraternity service projects and the corporate picnics. Wave to your young professional peers but keep it moving to where the old heads are congregating. Hang with your peers during hang time, not during "prime time." During prime time, find out where the established professionals are—you know, the class of '85 or '95 at the reunion or the vice president squeezing his brown mustard on the hot dog bun at the company picnic. Park there and start your conversations.

It will feel uncomfortable as hell for a while, but it will get easier over time and you'll gain more confidence as you practice connecting to more experienced pros. Put all of the tips you learned from the "Hugs & Handshakes" section into practice because the "old heads" are your goldmine. Those are the people most able and willing to open doors for you and advance your career, so invest in building those relationships whenever you have the chance.

You're probably becoming aware of this by now, but your peers are your competition. Young professionals are often comparing themselves to one another—who got promoted, who finished grad school, who got a signing bonus, who got cast in a part. As cool and friendly as some sincerely are, they may be far less generous with their resources and connections than the old heads.

Trust me.

Of course, this does not mean you neglect to cultivate your peer relationships; they are vital. But the mistake many young professionals make is they fail to get out of the comfort zone of their peer circle, not recognizing it's the old heads that will guide them to the pot at the end of the rainbow, metaphorically speaking.

Your friends and colleagues have good intentions, but the old heads often have good intentions *compounded with* influence and a desire to see "Little Timmy" (that's you) succeed. Remember, you're still in that cute, young professional stage, even at 29, though you may be trying your darnedest to prove you're on par with the pros that have gone before you. Slow your roll and seize the moment. Being "high-potential" is a good thing. Use it to your advantage while you can.

INSIDER SECRET #46
O.P.E.—Other People's Experience

"You want to learn from experience, but you want to learn from other people's experience when you can."
—WARREN BUFFETT, legendary business magnate and investor

You'll make a ton of mistakes across your lifetime. Some of them will be unavoidable encounters with destiny that will alter the course of your life in a good way. They might be painful, but you'll probably come out on the other side thankful for the better version of you that emerges as a result. Many mistakes you'll make, however, would have been totally avoidable had you asked better questions, been humble enough to apply the advice, done a bit more homework and paid attention to the signs in the fast lane toward your wrong direction.

So take this insider secret from Warren Buffet to heart: Learn from *other* people's experience when you can. It's true that everybody is different, and just because a situation turned out a certain way for one person doesn't mean it will turn out the same for you, but as peak performance coach Tony Robbins says, "Success leaves clues."

Screw-ups leave clues, too.

So as you zoom through the fast lane of your career or business, commit to first understanding other people's experiences, then learn from them. As you get to know your boss, your colleagues and other experienced professionals and entrepreneurs, find out what they've done well and what they would do differently in various areas of life and work. Here's a sample script:

> "May I ask you a question? I love to learn from other people and I'm always curious about what they've done well and what they would do differently. If you were giving your best advice to someone, what's one thing you've done really well in your career (or business, life, parenting, marriage, investing, etc. . . . pick ONE) that you would recommend someone emulate?"

—or—

> "May I ask you a question? I love to learn from other people and I'm always curious about what they've done well and what they would do

differently. If you were giving your best advice to someone, what's the one thing you've done in your career (or business, life, parenting, marriage, investing, etc. ... pick ONE) that you would have done differently, knowing what you know now?"

Most people like to give advice. They like to give advice even when they don't know what they're talking about, but they *love* to give advice when they do. And what topic do people know better than themselves—their opinions, their experiences, their points of view? Whoever you ask these questions to will be flattered that you did. Chances are you won't be able to get them to shut up!

This may come as a surprise to you, but at age 19, 20 or 25, you don't quite know everything (imagine that!), so don't discriminate on whom you're willing to learn from. Use this strategy with the vice president of your company and the janitor in your building. Ask these questions of people you are networking with about any topic you might be discussing at the time. You will glean best practices for what to do in your career, business, life, parenting, marriage, investing, etc., and, more importantly, what *not* to do. Then you can weigh that advice against your own circumstances and belief systems to see what resonates and what doesn't.

Motivational speaker Jim Rohn said, "We must all suffer from one of two pains: the pain of discipline or the pain of regret. The difference is discipline weighs ounces while regret weighs tons." Discipline yourself to learn from other people's experiences and avoid the pain of unnecessary regret.

INSIDER SECRET #47
Flip the Script

"Don't live up to your stereotypes."
—SHERMAN ALEXIE, poet

You're self-centered. You job hop. You're too technology-focused. You know it all. You're entitled. You won't pay your dues. You have no work ethic. You need constant affirmations of your overinflated self-esteem. You're afraid to leave the nest and get out on your own. ...

In case you've been hiding under a rock the past few years, young professionals, as a group, have a less than favorable reputation in the workplace. Part of that reputation is legitimately earned as I'm sure you can pinpoint at least one stereotypically entitled or narcissistic homie in your circle of friends.

The other reason you've earned this rep, quite frankly, is because you stand out. You don't accept your parents' status quo of living just to work. Work is important, but you know there's more to life. You've got big dreams and you're optimistic that you can make those dreams come true. You believe in making a difference in the world. You believe in bucking the system and finding better, faster ways to do just about everything, and that threatens the generations before you. To quote marketing guru Seth Godin once again, "Criticism comes to those who stand out."

No matter how you've earned the stereotype or whether it's totally fair, it's there and you have got to learn to manage perceptions in the workplace if you plan to succeed. As soon as you walk through the door, some co-workers will have their "Spidey senses" up, waiting for you to show yourself as the immature and borderline disrespectful being they have preconceived you to be! If you sink to their low expectations, even a small mistake can get blown out of proportion. On the other hand, if you understand the generational sensitivities, you can defy expectations and win over your skeptics.

Let me stress this is not the time for an "us-against-them" attitude. We all face stereotypes of some kind or another. Sometimes those stereotypes work in our favor; other times they don't. Whether we win or lose the prejudice game depends on how we "flip the script."

Many of my coaching clients are old enough to be my parents. When I walk into the office—a black female who (fortunately for now!) looks far younger than my actual age—I have to defy some people's lowered expectations on the value of the advice they'll receive from me. I recognize that, for some people (not all), I might trigger certain biases. I don't waste time worrying if those biases are right or wrong, fair or not. Instead, I simply defy their expectations.

I respect and honor their experience yet confidently provide solutions to better their career, business and life. I apply the insider secrets we discuss in this book on building rapport and connecting. I've also created a professional brand, on and offline, so that clients can develop a level of understanding upfront for what I can do for them. I've learned to flip the script and exceed their expectations of how someone "like me," whatever that means, should show up. Doing so has impacted my career more than any other strategy across the course of my life, and it will impact yours as well.

> ## *Conversations in the Fast Lane*
> ## *...on Milking Your Age!*
>
> ✓ Does your behavior feed the negative stereotypes of young professionals or do you defy people's expectations by how you conduct yourself in professional settings?
>
> ✓ List three people whose experiences you can learn from right now—for your career, business, college or life?
>
> ✓ How comfortable do you feel initiating relationships with more established professionals or entrepreneurs? Is it something you gravitate to or shy away from?
>
> ✓ Now that you realize experienced professional really want to help, how will it impact your willingness to ask for help?
>
> ✓ In what ways can you take greater advantage of your age right now?

As I was researching this topic, I came across a blog written by a young woman who was clearly fed up with the stereotypes of her generation. It was evident from the "up yours" attitude she gave off in her blog that anybody over 40 who might subscribe to negative millennial stereotypes could *suck it!* While I sympathized with her frustrations, she didn't win me over. In fact, she probably only succeeded in reinforcing those stereotypes by her stank attitude in defending against them!

There is a much better way. Singer songwriter Frank Ocean is quoted as saying, "Work hard in silence; let your success be your noise." Because you are younger, people have all kinds of preconceived notions on how you will dress in the workplace, how you will communicate, your work ethic, your professionalism, your ability to solve problems, your ability to handle criticism, your ability to handle pressure. This list can go on and on.

Unlike our blogger friend, you don't have to combat generational stereotypes in the workplace by confrontation and challenge. Instead, let your success be your noise. Show up opposite the misperceptions and defy the expectations. Diligently put into practice the secrets you've learned in this book, and because so few of your peers are doing so, you will stand out (in a good way!) and make an indelible impression on the very people who can influence your success. This is what it means to flip the script.

Remember, you cannot change a person's mind, but when you can change a person's experience, they'll change their own mind. How will people experience you?

> "Success and happiness are not matters of chance, but choice."
> — Zig Ziglar, author and motivational speaker

SECTION 11

••••

Happiness Matters

OVER THE YEARS, I have learned that people have a funny relationship with happiness. Some people focus on it more than others, but most people don't quite "get it." Driven achievers have a way of undervaluing happiness, delaying it, putting it off until the next big accomplishment. Insecure achievers resist happiness, feeling like they're undeserving and unworthy of it. Entitled achievers take happiness for granted, thinking the world lives and breathes just to make them happy. Few of us get this happiness thing right and even fewer get it right consistently.

The first thing you need to know about happiness is that happiness matters *now*. Happiness doesn't have to wait until you work through all your childhood trauma with your therapist. You don't need validation from your parents to be happy, nor do you need all your ducks in a row, all the stars to align, or all the people around you to get their acts together for you to be happy on your road to success.

No, you don't need any of those things, but make no mistake, this little gem ain't free. Happiness costs. It requires a unique kind of discipline and there are key secrets to make room for happiness that those of us older than you wish we knew years ago.

I don't know what makes you happy; heck, you might not know what makes you happy! But now is the time to start exploring and figuring it out—on the job, in your relationships, in your volunteer work and spiritual life. Find the experiences that truly make your heart sing, open your creativity, stretch your mind and imagination, and light your fire. Then use the strategies in this next section to bring more and more of that happiness into your life.

INSIDER SECRET #48
The Money Honey

"Do not save what is left after spending, but spend what is left after saving."
—WARREN BUFFETT, business magnate

This might be the most boring chapter in the book. I also believe it is the secret most of you will be inclined to ignore, either because you don't believe you make enough money now to save or because you have far more interesting things to do with your money than save it. After all, happiness *now* is what matters, right?

Yes, happiness matters now, and that's why saving matters now, as well. When we are young and starting to make our first "real money," nearly everything we want, every trip we could take, every cause we want to support, requires money. Real life isn't played with Monopoly money and if you don't believe me, take a peep at your student loan balance. How many years and how much per month is it going to take you to pay off that debt? Five years? Ten years?

Mercy.

So, saving money is not just about disciplining yourself for that retirement nest egg in 40 years. Retirement is important, but retiring could be the most distant thing from your mind right now. Instead, try looking at saving this way: Saving now will give you freedom whenever you need it.

When I was in my early 30s, I had gotten to a place where I absolutely hated my job. I was sick, tired, bored, burned out and a bit depressed. I seriously hated that job, and I had felt that way for a few years. Then it clicked one late night when I was leaving the office on my way home for the Christmas holiday. "Why am I doing this? I don't have to do this." At the time, I was not married. I didn't have kids. I had no debt outside of a house mortgage. I didn't *have* to work that job. I planned my exit strategy right then and there. I was quitting, baby!

…And six months later I was gone.

I spent the next year diving head-long into seminars, books, programs, and health and wellness retreats to find my passion and purpose. That time was the catalyst for me to become the woman I am now, doing exactly what I want to do with my life. I hired a tennis coach just for kicks and we'd practice early in the mornings in the city.

I remember watching people heading to the train or bus on their morning commute thinking, "Man – my life is kinda cool!"

How did that kinda cool life happen for me? I *saved*.

Now, of course I couldn't live that way forever. I had to eventually figure things out and begin to earn income again, but saving my money gave me options. When work got too unbearable, I had the freedom to leave. I had the freedom to try something different. I had the freedom to explore my passion and take risks. Some roads led to dead ends; others drove me right off the cliff when my first business failed, but saving money gave me a ticket to get into the fast lane of my own life and drive.

One of my few regrets is not investing more of my own time in learning how to manage my money when I was a young professional. I saved, yes, but I could have saved even more if I really understood this secret. When talking of saving, experts often say, "You've got to put away something for a rainy day," as if the only reason to save is in the event of personal calamity. That's certainly a valid reason, but this secret stresses saving for *freedom*, not failure.

So no matter if you're barely scraping by or making a pretty good chunk of change on your job, save a lot of your money—not because you have to, but because you *get* to.

For questions related to your portfolio, investment and retirement strategies, seek the counsel of a good financial advisor who's *walking their talk*, meaning they have some personal evidence of prospering from the same strategies they are recommending to you.

Author Genevieve Davis has a very effective strategy for managing your personal finances on a regular basis. I adopted that strategy for myself. Genevieve encourages people to create a "Rainy Day" fund, a Gratitude fund, a "Fun Time!" fund, and an Optional fund. The optional fund could be a "BIG! Dream" fund, which we'll talk about in the next chapter. It could be your "Debt-Free-by-33!" fund in the case of massive student loans or a "Wedding Bells" fund if you have sights set on getting married. Whatever it is, let the fourth fund represent a really fulfilling milestone for you.

With every paycheck or source of income, invest 10 percent of the gross earnings into your Rainy Day fund. For instance, if you earn $2000, 10 percent would be $200. That's your savings and you should not touch your savings unless there is a dire emergency. Needing an extra $300 to fly to Vegas with your friends *does not* constitute a dire emergency!

Then, invest a second 10 percent of the gross check into your gratitude fund. The gratitude fund is money you earmark to donate. Give that money to a charity, your church, a cause, a friend or stranger in need. Yes, *give it away*. Your generosity will come back to you in dividends when you least expect it.

Then, invest another 10 percent into your "Fun Time!" fund. You can do anything you want with that money, but it should be fun. Go out to dinner, hit up a concert, get your nails done, by a new pair of sneakers, take a weekend trip—whatever. That's the money you set aside to enjoy yourself.

Invest a final 10 percent into your optional fund—the "BIG! Dream" fund, the "Debt-Free-by-33" fund—or whatever you choose. The optional fund typically represents a big purchase or expenditure that will take some time to afford. Little by little, though, you can make a dent in that milestone.

What's great about managing your money by funds is that it doesn't matter how much money you make, you can do this. If you're starting out, you might only have enough to invest $20 in each fund. That's okay. What that means is that you may only get to spend $20 for a weekend of fun because that's all you have in your Fun Time! account, instead of the $60 you might have been tempted to charge on your credit card, incurring debt.

If you start banking your Fun Time! money like old school "rollover minutes," you have the freedom to do more expensive things. Either way, you're creating freedom in your budget to enjoy spending your money whatever way brings you the highest gratification. At the same time, you're saving in case something unexpected happens while taking baby steps toward a meaningful (though expensive) long-term goal through whatever optional fund you create.

To be clear, the 10 percent standard is a ballpark metric. If you live in an expensive city like San Francisco or New York and you're interning or just starting out, 10 percent might be impossible for you. If you have a family to care for, your household expenses might not support a 10 percent contribution across all four funds.

If that's the case, lower your percentage to 5 percent or vary the percentage for each fund based on your priorities. For instance, your Rainy Day fund might get 10 percent but your Big Dream! fund might only get 3 percent. Just make the percentages doable for you. The point is to be consistent, even if only a little bit at a time. If you are diligent with the small amount, opportunities will open for you to contribute more over time.

Sure, saving may mean fewer expensive dinners or concerts on a whim, but I mentioned in the opening chapter that happiness ain't free. Someday (likely sooner than you expect) you're going to want to do something pretty sweet and your ability to do that sweet thing will largely depend on whether or not you have the money. Do yourself a favor and take this secret to heart:

Saving now gives you freedom…*whenever you want it.*

INSIDER SECRET #49
Your Next Big Thing

"The key is not to prioritize what's on your schedule, but to schedule your priorities."
—STEPHEN COVEY, American educator and author

Happiness gets…scheduled? Yep. Scheduled.

If you're one of those who loves (or at least used to love) adventure, fun and community service, make it a habit to plan those experiences into your life. When you come off your vacation, immediately schedule your next one. Where do you want to go? Who do you want to go with? Look at your city's entertainment calendar, find an entertainer who is coming to town and make it an outing with your friends. Schedule a long weekend and go visit your parents out of the blue. You don't have to pay for it now, but at least you'll have a goal and vision to strive for what excites you.

In the mad dash to succeed, many people miss the magic moments of happiness along the way. As you enter the workforce, you won't have the luxury of being as spontaneous as you used to be, and if you're not careful, the urgent (work and responsibilities) will often take precedence over the important, more meaningful experiences in your life. So, a big insider secret to happiness on the road to success is to deliberately plan your next big thing.

And that's where the Big Dream! fund from the last chapter comes into play. If you have been putting a few bucks into your dream fund, you'll have the money to do really cool things without charging on credit cards or living beyond your means. You won't get that pit in your stomach at the group dinner when splitting the bill nine ways costs more than what you actually ate and can comfortably pay for!

In case you haven't figured it out by now, the next big thing isn't the next big achievement; it's your next big moment…or little moment. Whatever fills your happiness tank.

INSIDER SECRET #50
Celebrate Small Wins

"Small daily micro wins, when done continually over time, lead to staggering results."
—ROBIN SHARMA, author

Graduating from law school…big moment. Getting promoted to manager…big moment. Launching your first product…big moment. Getting married…*B.I.G.* moment!

In the real world, you don't hop from one big moment to the next. In fact, the bigger your goals, the more time you'll spend in between the big wins, doing "regular stuff" that, when compounded, result in a pretty extraordinary life. A highly underrated secret to success is choosing to celebrate the small wins that result from doing the regular stuff over and over. It may seem to some like a "hokey" practice, but if you plan to make it to the mountaintop in your career or business, you must learn to pat yourself on the back for achieving the mini milestones.

When I first wrote the *Fast Lane, Wrong Direction* professional edition, I interviewed an accomplished female entrepreneur, Sophie. When I asked her about one of the biggest challenges in building her business at the start, she shared:

"Nothing is ever enough. The focus is on the next big thing! When you hit it, there's no time to celebrate; it's on to the next big deal! I'm not only that way at work. I didn't go to my grad school graduation. It wasn't a big deal to me. I marvel at people who are genuinely able to celebrate things."

Notice this wasn't just a business issue for Sophie, it was a mindset issue. Though only 8 percent of Americans age 25-29 had completed graduate degrees in 2014, according to the National Center for Education Statistics, Sophie didn't think the accomplishment was worth the time to attend the ceremony!?! Her mind was focused on the next big achievement, and that same mindset plagued the early stages of her business, making her a pretty unhappy chick even though she was doing some cool things with her work.

You will have moments on your journey when you're working for the very organization you want to work for doing exactly what you set out to do, yet you'll find yourself questioning what the hell you signed up for! In those moments, the road to success may not feel like success at all and your next big win may be nowhere in sight. In those moments, blow up the small wins—debugging the code the first time around, getting a call back for the audition or securing lunch with a potential mentor. Every one of those wins matters.

Remember, true success isn't just about the big achievements; enjoying the ride along the way is pretty darn important. Take it from Sophie.

INSIDER SECRET #51
Invest in Experiences

"The purpose of life is to live it, to taste experience to the utmost, to reach out eagerly and without fear for newer and richer experience."
—ELEANOR ROOSEVELT, former First Lady, diplomat, activist

If you truly want to look back on your young professional years with no regret, spend your new money on experiences, not just things. Save as we discussed in earlier chapters but also travel, make memories, have cool experiences, impact people's lives. Most young professionals are making more money than they have made their entire life, yet some waste that money on the latest tech gadgets, expensive cars and high-end living. Don't misunderstand me, there's no need to "slum it out." But expensive things are material things—they break, wear out, get stolen, sold and lost. Clothes fade, shrink, rip and most times aren't nearly as cute as they looked when you absolutely "had" to buy them on sale.

A great example of the benefit of investing in experiences is my husband's good friend, Dino. Dino recently celebrated his 40th birthday, and as a gift, his girlfriend decided to create a photo scrapbook of his life. She asked his friends, family, old college mates, fraternity brothers, colleagues, mentors, mentees, etc. to submit pictures and birthday wishes from across the years. The gift turned out to be this huge book full of old photos from their travels—Venezuela, Argentina, Thailand, bachelor parties, summer picnics, football games, road trips.

You see, Dino, my husband and their crew have traveled to some destination,

Conversations in the Fast Lane
. . . on Happiness Matters

✓ "Take the time to enjoy being a young person. You'll never get that time back." —*Tracy, senior consultant, New Jersey*

✓ "Find yourself on the simple level. Find the little kid you thought you had to leave behind because you're now an 'adult.' Incorporate the openness, wonder and joys of your inner kid into your life." —*Justice, real estate investor, Maryland*

✓ "At 21, I had taken good values from my parents as it related to saving money. I definitely recommend you learn how to save." —*Vicki, entrepreneur, Pennsylvania*

✓ "Ask, ask and ask again how to do what you want. Ask everybody, even those you think don't know the answer, because your answers may come from the most unlikely sources." —*Courtney, psychologist, California*

✓ "You don't have to be a lawyer at 25. You don't have to be a doctor at 29. You can take a year to explore who you are, what you want to do and not necessarily get caught in grad school so soon. I understand a lot of people say that when you take a year off school, it's really hard to get re-motivated. That's true, but do you know how hard it is to get re-motivated when you're 35 and hate your job?!?" —*Bruce, video game developer, California*

---

domestic or abroad, nearly every year since they graduated. At this point, they're at about 15 trips and counting. Across the years, these guys were all starting new jobs, going to grad school, med school, residencies, starting businesses, in-between jobs, etc. But for some reason, they made commitments to invest in their experiences. Sometimes these were cheap trips, and as money flowed better, they had "less cheap" trips. The point is, Dino is able to look back on a short lifetime of remarkable experiences.

Dino now makes great money as a geneticist. He has invested in a house and drives a nice car, but he will be the first to tell you that, in his youth, he would spend his hard-earned money on experiences before material things any day.

You don't have to have a big crew of friends nor do you need wild adventures in Argentina to invest in your own experiences. Your wild adventure may be a mission trip to your inner city rec center or a coupon for a local trapeze class. You don't have to overthink it to create magic moments in your success, but you do have to prioritize how you invest.

> "You only live once, but if you live right,
> once is enough."
> — Mae West, legendary actress

CLOSING

····

It's Just a Game

I **WILL ADMIT** that I'm late to the YOLO craze, and I'm not convinced we've only got one life to live, but I think Mae West's sentiment captures the essence of this book. Realize this can be the time of your life. Ten years from now, when you have some life experience under your belt and you're much more established in your work, that, too, can be the time of your life. Twenty years from now, when you're raising kids and in the groove of family, that can be the time of your life, as well.

Your ability to enjoy the time of your life at every stage hinges on whether or not you're willing to pay the price of finding and maintaining your right direction at that stage. For some, "right direction" means figuring out your next career move. For others, it's having the same confidence in yourself that other people think you have.

Still for others, "right direction" means getting more visible and stepping out of the comfort zone of your current level of achievement.

We all experience emotional highs at a moment of a breakthrough, and I sincerely hope that you have had quite a few breakthroughs through the course of our time together. But just when you think you've cracked the right direction code in one area of your life, something will inevitably happen that challenges your belief in these principles. Why? Because right direction often feels like a test, then another test… and another test…and in some ways it actually is.

That's how the game of success works. You understand success is a game, right?

And what all of us who are cheering for you want to know is whether or not you'll win. Winning any game, especially when you're graduating from the amateur league and turning pro, boils down to three main questions:

1.) Do You Know the Game?
Equipping you to know the rules of the game of success as you embark on your professional adventure is the entire point of this book. So, if you have gotten this far, you know the game and you can always come back to the rules book as you evolve. Depending on where you are in your professional journey, some points will be essential for you right now and others will make even more sense as your career progresses. Either way, you've got the insider secrets to achieve anything you want out of your life right now.

2.) Can You Play the Game?
This question now points to your skill. Knowing that you should do something is one thing; being *able* to do it is completely different. Hopefully, you have discovered new skills in our journey together that you had no clue about before. Master those skills! I have no doubt you absolutely suck at some of those skills now, so you likely can't play the game of success *well* because you haven't yet mastered the skills. However, that doesn't mean you can't play at all.

You are living proof that you have the ability to learn anything you set your mind to, and learning how to implement any of the insider secrets that don't come naturally to you is no exception. So, if you need to get over your fear of starting conversations with people so that you can master Hugs & Handshakes, you can learn how to do that. There are so many books on networking and building professional relationships. Local business associations and alumni groups also host trainings on networking. There are plenty of ways to improve in this area; simply ask people around you for resources.

Can you learn how to manage your online brand, model the best in others, find your passion, exceed expectations, bloom where you're planted, and watch your mouth? Yes, yes, yes, yes, yes and yes.

So, yes, you *can* play the game of success. You may play it awkwardly in the beginning as your skills improve. But if Michael Jordan could fail his way to becoming an NBA Hall of Fame basketball player after getting cut from his high school team, you can fail your way to success, too.

3.) Are You Willing to Play the Game?
Only you can answer this question, and it's the most important question of all. You have been equipped with some powerful tools in these chapters. These are the insider secrets—the strategies, mindset and principles—established profes-

sionals wish they knew at the start of their careers to do work they love and truly thrive in it. These are the hidden secrets that convert internships to full-time job offers and catapult you leaps and bounds beyond your peers in the workplace. Just as importantly, these insider secrets will help you enjoy the ride on the road to success.

You must decide if you're willing to try them, willing to master them and willing to be uncomfortable for a long, long while as these tools transform who you are as a professional. This wisdom will do absolutely nothing for you if you do nothing with it.

You are turning pro and the game of success is about to change for you—*fast*. But you have got everything you need to change with it. There is absolutely no limit to what you can achieve, experience and enjoy in your work and life. With that, I'll leave you with three parting instructions:

Be brilliant. Be dazzling. Be You!

About the Author and Speaker

Renessa Boley Layne is creator of the Success and Happiness Test and author of *Fast Lane, Wrong Direction: Insider Secrets to Redesign Your Success and Reclaim Your Passion, Purpose and Balance You Lost Along the Way*. Renessa speaks at colleges, companies and associations to help young and established professionals alike to experience "fast lane, *right direction*" in their career, leadership and personal life design. Renessa's coaching programs equip people to discover, design and get highly paid to do work they love.

Renessa is a dynamic speaker and has appeared as a leading authority on ABC, CBS, NBC and Fox TV affiliates across the country. She has also been featured in publications such as Career Builder, CNN.com, Heart & Soul magazine and Washington Post. She holds an Industrial Engineering degree from Stanford University and brings 20 years of corporate and entrepreneurial success to her training. You can learn more about her at www.renessaspeaks.com.

> *Renessa simply dazzles! She's a huge value-add to any audience. I highly recommend her.*
> —Terrence Noonan, 5-Time Emmy Award-winning producer

Renessa is available as a keynote speaker on:
- Life and Career Design
- Career Development and Promotion
- Leadership and Team Building
- Strategic Networking and Influence
- Transition to Entrepreneurship
- Success: From College to the Real World
- Performance, Productivity and Professional Presence

To schedule Renessa to speak at your next event:
Visit: www.renessapeaks.com
Email: hello@renessaspeaks.com

Made in the USA
San Bernardino, CA
11 September 2017